REJECTION
FREE™

HOW TO CHOOSE YOURSELF FIRST
AND TAKE CHARGE OF YOUR LIFE
BY CONFIDENTLY ASKING FOR
WHAT YOU WANT

**REJECTION
FREE FOR
LIFE SERIES**

SCOTT ALLAN

Rejection Free

HOW TO CHOOSE YOURSELF FIRST AND TAKE
CHARGE OF YOUR LIFE BY CONFIDENTLY
ASKING
FOR WHAT YOU WANT

Books by Scott Allan

Empower Your Thoughts

Drive Your Destiny

<u>Relaunch Your Life</u>

The Discipline of Masters

Do the Hard Things First

Undefeated

No Punches Pulled

Fail Big

Rejection Free

Built for Stealth

Check out the complete collection of books and training here:

www.scottallanbooks.com

Start Reading

Rejection
Free

HOW TO CHOOSE YOURSELF FIRST AND TAKE
CHARGE OF YOUR LIFE BY CONFIDENTLY
ASKING
FOR WHAT YOU WANT

Scott Allan

www.scottallanbooks.com

www.scottallanbooks.com

ISBN 978-1-989599-00-6 (paperback)

ISBN 978-1-989599-01-3 (hardcover)

ISBN 978-1-989599-18-1 (ebook)

Contents

"Perhaps we shall learn, as we pass through this age, that the 'other self' is more powerful than the physical self we see when we look in the mirror."

— **Napoleon Hill,** *author of Think and Grow Rich*

Living the Rejection Free Journey

"Confront the dark parts of yourself, and work to banish them with illumination and forgiveness. Your willingness to wrestle with your demons will cause your angels to sing.

— **August Wilson,** American Playwright

First of all, I want to do two things: I want to **welcome you** into this book *Rejection Free* and, say **thank you**. You have just made a positive step in taking charge of your life and I am happy to have you here.

I wrote this book because I know the power that rejection plays in all of our lives. If it is allowed to operate unhinged, rejection can control our choices and influence our decisions. If allowed to go unattended, rejection eventually kills our dreams.

You might live in fear of rejection as I had for many decades. But it doesn't have to be that way. In this book I show you that you can win against your fears, rise up to become anything you want, and do whatever you like without living in fear. Whatever rejection issues you have can and will be overcome. I want you to know that you are not alone on this journey.

Fear of rejection can be a very isolating emotion. In order to protect ourselves, we covet our emotions and stay hidden, like small children underneath the blankets afraid of the dark. We try to "play it safe" and take less risks.

The problem with this is that we give up on life-changing opportunities, ideas, and chances in order to avoid the pain rejection brings. This pain not only causes emotional trauma but also can be, for many of us, just as frightening as facing physical injury or even death.

As rejectees, we become like chameleons in a large jungle: we fear being spotted by the predators, so we become adept at blending in, transforming, and disappearing. Ashamed to show ourselves for who we really are, we reject ourselves by staying out of sight. If they can't find you, they can't judge or condemn.

The jungle is the perfect place to avoid attracting attention. This means less social pressure. We can stay below the radar without being asked to do anything outside of our comfort zone. By staying out of sight, you avoid being judged or criticized. We have adapted to a lifestyle that has become our survival zone.

Many of us have convinced ourselves that life is better this way. By hiding from painful situations where the possibility of being judged, ridiculed, or condemned is present, we can control our environment through avoidance. This is not a way to live but a method of survival.

Let me ask you this: What chances or dreams have you given up to stay hidden away? What do you regret not doing because the fear of being ostracized or turned down was just too much to face?

Being rejected is a very real experience. For those people who have attached a deeper, more personal emotion to rejection, it can be completely terrifying.

Consider these questions:

- *What would you do right now if you removed your fear of rejection? What acceptable risks would you take? What opportunities would you explore?*

- *What would you succeed at and commit to if you could remove your feelings of shame? What ideas would you pursue? What would you create?*

- *How can you see your life transforming by pushing through your personal pain of rejection?*

- *Can you imagine a life in which you could be free of your rejection issues once and for all?*

- *Do you struggle with people pleasing, only to end up more alone and confused?*

- *How often do you challenge your fear of being put on the spot?*

- *Do you turn down opportunities for speaking engagements?*

- *Do you stay in relationships because you are afraid of taking a chance on something or someone new?*

- *Do you refrain from asking for the things you really want for fear of being told NO?*

Rejection is not exclusive to any one person or group of individuals. It is something we all go through. The difference is in how we deal with it.

For years I avoided any situation that put my ego-sensitive self at risk. If I was denied something I wanted, it was a personal attack on my character. When someone criticized me or made a disparaging remark, it was because I deserved it for being a "less-than." By making it personal, I became more fearful. As we will see later in this book, rejection comes in many forms and disguises.

In *Rejection Free*, we will learn the specific strategies for how to:

- Choose yourself first, no matter what people think of you

- Ask for what you want without the fear of hearing *NO*

- Break free of rejection in any situation that calls for you to be brave and confront your fears

- Stop trying to please the wrong people and pay attention to the right ones

- Realize that rejection isn't all about you (and how inspiring this is!)

- Put an end to the trap of predictability and the ways it hurts your chances for success.

- Overcome your self-doubt and become great at asking for what you want the most.

- Supercharge your confidence and take charge of your life.

- Desensitize yourself to rejection, so that you can handle anything that comes your way!

Rejection happens to all of us. Nobody is immune to it. However, every time rejection tries to defeat you, you can use the techniques and strategies in this book to defeat rejection instead. You can learn to free yourself from the feeling of shame and the fear of loss. By taking action in the face of fear, you release yourself from an emotional rollercoaster and learn to live your life with confidence.

Now, just to be clear, this book isn't about how to avoid rejection. *Rejection Free* is designed to put you in charge of your life by dealing with life's situations when you *are* faced with rejection.

When we have developed the life skills for handling fearful situations, we can move away from retreat and take action. This book will teach you how to take your experience of rejection and turn it into every advantage.

Here are some examples of rejection at work in daily life:

- You ask for a raise or vacation at work and your manager says *NO*, your performance level has been below average.

- You finally get up the courage to ask out that girl you've been watching for the last six months … and then she walks past you on the street with another guy.

- The new book you just published has four reviews, and three of them are negative.

- The bank says *NO* to your loan application because you don't make enough money.

- The dream job you're banking on getting is awarded to someone younger.

- You ask someone for help and they say *NO*.

- Your spouse that you've been married to for twenty years suddenly files for divorce.

- Your presentation you've worked on for months has people walking out.

Building the Rejection Free Lifestyle

I'm inviting you to join me on a journey: It's a journey to a greater sense of freedom. It's a guided plan to provide you with the techniques and deeper awareness to deal with rejection, instead of trying to escape and avoid it. We can't escape from it, but we *can* free ourselves from falling into self-pity and going through the pain of regret for missed opportunities later on in life.

Over the years I have discovered that taking less risks to avoid rejection is not an escape plan but instead, it can become a path to failing quietly. Less risk equals less of everything. The risks I am talking about are the opportunities that we let slip and ignore for fear of losing what we have.

But, it doesn't have to be this way.

There *is* a solution. It is not as difficult as you may think. The way out for you is so close, you are almost there. But you will have to take action and get your hands dirty.

Your other option is to continue living in fear. If you are reading this book, I assume you want the tools to handle rejection and **be free** of the power it has over you.

Breaking out of your fear-based comfort zone—your protective cocoon—isn't always easy, but it's definitely possible. If it were easy, we would all be doing it. But good things come to those that try and persevere.

People do it every day. Look around you. Find someone that has recently succeeded at something.

We have this opinion that all the successful people out there are somehow better than we are. They have tons of confidence and support and on the outside, it appears that their success is guaranteed.

But, this just isn't true.

People who get to where they want to go do so by pushing through their fear. History is filled with many successful entrepreneurs, authors, actors, and musicians who struggled with rejection for years and multiple times before they made it to where they wanted to be.

Harland David Sanders, better known as Colonel Sanders of Kentucky Fried Chicken, had a hard time selling his chicken at first. His famous secret chicken recipe was rejected 1,009 times before a restaurant finally accepted it.

Charlie Chaplin was initially rejected by Hollywood studio chiefs because they thought his style of comedy and acting was too nonsensical to ever be popular or entertaining.

A newspaper editor fired **Walt Disney** because "he lacked imagination and had no good ideas." After that, Disney started a number of businesses that ended with bankruptcy and failure. Pushing through and moving forward, Disney's "lack of imagination" created a billion-dollar empire that is enjoyed by millions of children and adults every year.

Albert Einstein, who did not speak until he was four and couldn't read until he was seven, was expelled from school and was refused admittance to the Zurich Polytechnic School. Teachers and parents believed he was slow and mentally handicapped. Einstein went on to win the Nobel Prize and his work and theories changed the face of modern physics.

One of the most successful TV talents in history, and one of the richest women in the world, **Oprah Winfrey** was fired from as a television reporter for being "unfit" for TV.

In this book we are going to learn to:

- **Take action** when you are afraid.

- **Take action** to break the specific fear of rejection.

- **Take action** when you are paralyzed and feel helpless to do anything.

- **Desensitize** your fear of rejection by doing what scares you.

You may be thinking, "But what action should I take? You say 'take action' like it is an easy thing to do. I would take action, but I don't know where to take action first."

Let's take this one step at a time. First of all, we start with small steps. You don't have to jump into the ocean and expect to swim to the other side of the Atlantic right away, but you do have to at least get your feet wet.

Take small actions every day toward defeating something that scares you and rejection loses its power. In the end, this is what we want: to reduce the power of your fear-based self; to empower you to build a new mindset that strips away all self-doubt.

This can be done. You can do it.

If you are willing to risk yourself by putting the "real you" out there, you could end up creating a specific situation that changes your life significantly. When you take action and do what scares you the most, you are taking charge of your life and your destiny.

By not risking, you risk more. By hiding, you stay afraid.

When you isolate yourself from your pain, as we often do, it amplifies the pain of being alone and heightens the experience of rejection. There is risk in everything. There is risk in doing *nothing* and risk in doing *something*. There are consequences and rewards to everything. We win and we fail at times. Let's stay focused on winning together and breaking free of the emotional chains keeping you trapped.

The ball is in your court.

It's time to play.

PART 1:
Choose Yourself First.

CHAPTER 1

Debunking the Lies of Rejection

"I know that when a door closes, it can feel like all doors are closing. A rejection letter can feel like everyone will reject us. But a closed door leads to clarity. It's really an arrow. Because we cannot go through that door, we will go somewhere else. That somewhere else is your true life."

— Tama J. Kieves

Rejection is full of lies we believe about ourselves. One of the first steps to recovery and creating a rejection-free lifestyle is breaking away from these lies by becoming totally honest with ourselves. Aligning our thoughts and ideals with the reality of the situation makes less resistance for ourselves.

These lies keep us from achieving the happiness and freedom we *could* have. **The lies are what keep you trapped** and continue the pattern of living in **rejection hell**. This is a term I coined for when we are so fearful of rejection because of our insecurities that we walk around expecting it from everyone.

As long as you are acting, behaving, and thinking differently than the person you want to be, you keep living out these lies every day.

Lies, Myths and Half-Truths

For the most part I always believed that there was something wrong with me, that my rejection was an illness that only I had contracted; the rest of the world was perfect and I was flawed. But when you question this logic you can start to see the lies behind the fractured belief.

We all buy into the lies that perpetuate and support this condition. If you convince yourself that you are not good enough, you'll always be trying to prove yourself to someone. Even after having some big wins under your belt, you'll chalk it up to "I was just lucky."

We are flawed in the sense that we have a hard time accepting ourselves as we are; there is this obsession to want to be more, have more, or prove that we do have worth and value. But it's like trying to fill up a bucket with a hole in the bottom.

Big Lie #1: I have to agree with everyone and value his or her opinion above all else.

When you agree with everyone, you don't agree with anyone. You are looking to make friends and please everyone on both sides of the fence; when people find out that you'll just say whatever they want to hear, nobody is going to value your opinion or pay attention to you. What'll happen is that you'll end up rejected again, only this time through your own doing.

We want to be liked, valued, and to be recognized as having a place in this world. But the base truth is that not everyone is going to like you. They might only want something from you such as a favor, so the buy-in you get from temporary kindness doesn't always last.

When you start thinking long-term and support those people who are your real friends, you can stop pretending to be popular and focus on being yourself." By focusing on delivering value to people, we attract the kind of friends and relationships that matter.

Big Lie #2: Getting rejected is personal and it means there is something wrong with me.

The power of a rejection is only as strong as you decide it should be. Two people can be rejected for the same thing: one person takes it personally and gives up; the other says, "Okay, who's next?" and keeps going. You have to keep going if you want to break free.

It doesn't matter if you ask someone out and they say *NO*. It doesn't matter if you apply for twenty jobs and they all say *NO*. It doesn't matter if you write a book and thirty publishers kick it out the door. That rejection you experience that basically says, "You're no good" either makes you or it breaks you. In the end, how you perceive the experience has everything to do with how you'll respond to it. "Rejection" is your opinion (your own judgment of your experience) and not anyone else's.

If someone doesn't like your character, or the way you look or act, just remind yourself these same people are not perfect either. Have you ever rejected someone? Think back to a time that you did and then figure out why. It is that belief at the heart of all this—that "I am inferior to the rest of the world" belief—that keeps us trapped in a rejected state.

Later in the book we will dive into this more, but one of the greatest lies about rejection that everyone buys into is that it is personal. It is the "I wasn't chosen because there is something wrong with me" syndrome. In most cases, what looks and feels personal actually has to do with the other party and not you at all.

There are times, painfully so, when we get rejected for personal reasons. We are too tall, not educated enough or we just don't have the right personality for the job.

But in many situations, we are rejected for reasons beyond our control that has more to do with the other person. The person rejecting you has his or her own personal reasons that extend beyond us. In fact, as I have experienced and what initially perceived as a personal attack on my character was a decision made by someone else based loosely on emotion.

So, take comfort in knowing that, regardless what painful rejection you have been through, we can't always control or be responsible for the decisions of others.

Big Lie #3: Rejection is a permanent condition that I was born with.

Everyone is at a different stage of the process regarding his or her rejection issues. For many, it lasts through high school and then they outgrow it; on the other hand, some people live with it their whole lives. But until you have faced and dealt with your fear of rejection, you will always be afraid of getting ousted or being told *NO*. For many, fear of rejection exists as a permanent condition if untreated.

If you grew up in a home that was critical, harsh, and controlling, your rejection issues are deep and could stick with you throughout your life, resulting in perfectionistic behavior and thinking that keeps the cycle going. Ongoing criticism damages your self-esteem and undermines your confidence at an early age.

If you went through this, your rejection issues will be unlikely to go away until you take action and do the things that you are now afraid to do. Rejection isn't permanent for anyone; sometimes you get a *YES* and many times you don't. Nobody is exempt. What makes all the difference is your reaction to a rejection moment.

Do you believe that you were born rejected? Or do you see it as something you contracted, like a virus that has no cure? The message I will share with you now and throughout this book is: **People are as rejected as they make up their minds to be.**

You can control the outcome of any situation where rejection is an issue. You have a choice to let it defeat you or empower you.

Big Lie #4: I'm different and weird and that's why I am being rejected.

Everyone is weird in his or her own unique way. When we try too hard to be normal it puts stress and pressure on us to perform. You were taught that there is such a thing as "normal" in this world, but that's a lie. There isn't any norm. This leads to perfectionistic thinking. You are not being rejected for being different.

You are being rejected by yourself because you're trying too hard to be something you are not; you are trying too hard to be "normal," a word used by people who are too afraid to be themselves. The next time you look at something and label it as weird, it could just be that you are sizing it up to fit with your own "normal" version of reality.

Your rejection persona is obsessed with "normalcy." It has its own built-in "normal" radar, so when you start acting or doing anything that is out of the ordinary, it sets off red flags and pulls you back. You might feel embarrassed or humiliated when you do something that is weird. You may not be aware of it, because you have been trying to act normal most of your life.

When you are heavily criticized for being you, over the years you become conditioned to not act strangely—it's not acceptable. "Normal people do this." "Normalcy is this way." It's a lie. There is conformity and as long as you are conforming to someone else's vision of how you should be behaving and acting, you'll throw aside your uniqueness and settle for boring over unique.

Big Lie #5: If only I were better, smarter, and more likeable, or, The Self-Rejection Persona.

You need to differentiate between the projections others put on you and what is actual fact. I know the world we live in appears differently. We see supermodels, rock stars, and actors buying lavish homes and getting hordes of attention. We feel cheated. *Where is my share? Why was I born differently?* As a friend of mine once said to me, "You can't be like Jeff Bezos. There is only one Jeff Bezos, and the job is taken." He was right. The best we can hope for is to be true to ourselves.

For years I compared myself to other people. Not happy with who I was, I wanted to be anyone else but **me**. I thought I was the problem. But in thinking this way, you reject yourself before anyone else can.

If only I had what he had …

If only I could be in his position …

If only I were good enough to …

Why is this happening to me again?

Why am I always excluded?

There, you see? I got turned down again …

These expectations we have created are not of our own making. We are trying to fulfill the expectations placed on us in our childhood. Do you remember? The pressure to perform, to be better, and to try harder so you didn't disappoint someone, most likely an older sibling or your parents.

As long as you are trying to fulfill the expectations you think others have, you're still living the same pattern over and over. You are trying to recreate what you failed at in the past. Only now, instead of trying to make someone else happy—which you know is impossible—you have put the pressure on yourself.

Self-expectations are the most damaging, because we don't realize that we are the ones who are setting the bar for ourselves. We have convinced ourselves that it's somebody else that expects this of us.

Big Lie #6: I can't succeed because I keep getting rejected, and rejection is a sign that I should give up and pursue something else.

You have the right to be yourself. By choosing yourself instead of rejecting who you are, the big lies are cast aside. What lies are those? *I am not worthy or I am not capable of being or doing what I feel passion about. I don't deserve to get recognition. I am odd and socially awkward.*

All lies. Sure, maybe they have some truth: Maybe you *are* socially awkward. Maybe you *are* lacking in a certain area of life that needs developing. Maybe you *do* have self-esteem issues. But who doesn't have these flaws? Growing up, there were people close to us who rejected us for our imperfections, and this has carried over to our adult lives. But now we still believe that rejection exists because we aren't good enough or are somehow inferior.

Remember what Henry Ford said: "Whether you think you can, or you think you can't—you're right."

What you think and believe becomes who you are. You will act on your thoughts and make your beliefs real. By giving up every time you go through a rejection, whether it is personal or in business, you are closing the doors on success

The key is to push through the fear and adapt to the pain. This might sound like "motivational hype" but it is the sure-fire strategy that works. Later on, we will look at the strategy for desensitization and how you can make yourself stronger, better, and more adept at handling anything that comes your way.

It takes time to work through these lies we have about ourselves. But as we move through this book and you have time to reflect on what you are learning, you will start to see a new set of truths emerge.

Our thoughts and beliefs have been corrupted over the years. By rejecting who we are, we have failed to become who we most wanted to be. This is the highest form of self-rejection.

Spend twenty minutes a day in silence. Schedule this time in if you need to. Explore your feelings and thoughts during this time. Question the beliefs you have about yourself. Try to see the lies through the negative emotions you are holding on to. Committing to a daily habit of self-exploration can open up your awareness and encourage you to transform the lies keeping you trapped.

"Always bear in mind that your resolution to succeed is more important than any other thing."

— **Abraham Lincoln**

CHAPTER 2

Choosing a Life Over a Life of Rejection

"We shouldn't romanticize rejection. There's nothing romantic about rejection. It's horrible."

— **Marlon James**

A mentor of mine once said to me, "If you want to make any serious changes in your life, you need to create a vision of the person you would most like to be. This has to be someone you admire and look up to. Someone you would like to be friends with and model yourself after. Someone who inspires you. Create that persona and then put all your efforts into becoming that person."

And so ...

I created Bob.

What About Bob?

Bob hates his job. He hates his life.

He has been working in the same office for fifteen years and lives a menial existence. He comes into work, punches in, punches out, and then, at the end of the day, he goes home to a small one-bedroom apartment. He watches a lot of television and tries not to think about things.

Bob has lost a lot of hope over the years. At times, he even thinks he doesn't have much to live for. Yet Bob has never tried to find a different job. He's never tried to change things, because he has chosen to accept life on life's terms, and retreats from reality.

Bob has never tried anything else that could make him happier. He never takes any chances or tries to meet new people. Bob lives a menial existence, and the worst part is, he knows it.

Every day is the same thing, day in and day out, even though he hates it. It makes no sense. His wife left him because he was so miserable. He lost many friends when he became cynical and down on life.

You see, Bob is terrified of being rejected. That is why he has never tried to succeed at anything else and avoids taking chances where there are no guarantees. For Bob, staying in a *predictable* situation, however painful, is better than going out there and taking the risk of being shot down. By anyone. By everyone.

Bob was rejected a lot in his earlier years. He never did well at school and rarely tried new things. In sports, Bob was chosen last to be on any team. If he asked women out, they would laugh at him before turning him down. He had low grades at school, and that carried over into almost every aspect of his life.

Over the years, Bob has developed a "rejection complex" in his relationship with the world. So, eventually, one day he decides that he won't be rejected anymore. One day, Bob just decides that he has had enough. He wants to live differently. He wants to be the person he dreamed of when he was a kid: passionate, excited, and ready to take on the world.

So, Bob does something completely irrational, unexpected and totally unplanned for. This turning point comes when a friend of his finally intervenes and says, "You are afraid because you create your own fear. You are unhappy because you choose to be unhappy. You fail because you believe in failure."

So, Bob makes an *actionable* decision: Bob decides one day that he is going to choose himself above everything else regardless of what other people think of him. He decides that instead of running from his fear, he will embrace it and use it as an opportunity to learn. Instead of playing it safe and risking nothing, he will take a chance on anything that challenges him, even if it means looking stupid.

Recognizing how he himself has created his own misery through buying into his "rejection persona," Bob goes out into the world. He is scared at first, but he takes action. He meets new people. He takes charge of his life in ways he never dreamed, instead of having life control him.

If he isn't good at certain sports, he finds a sport he *is* good at and excels in it. If there are certain women that laugh at him or don't think he is good enough, he finds the woman of his dreams and just says "To hell with the rest."

When Bob fails to get into a university because of his low marks in school, he doesn't just settle for a low-paying, minimum-wage job; he teaches himself new skills and creates his own work online, selling courses and doing what he loves.

Now, when Bob faces rejection, he turns it into a positive experience by not buying into the expectations that he once imagined the world had toward him. This way, Bob forges his own future. In time, he makes a new set of friends who support his ventures, and he supports theirs.

Bob has changed. He is finally free.

Unlike Bob, most people who still live in fear of what they can't do are trapped in a cycle of rejection that they live to regret.

But how does Bob do this? He doesn't let the world dictate his worth. He laughs at people when they say he is crazy for trying something they normally won't. He does what others say can't be done. Bob has a mission that he is clear about: *"Do the things you've only dreamed of doing, and when you are done, go do more of that."*

Yes, Bob has fear, but he also has something more: conviction. He knows what he wants. He works hard to get it. Despite the obstacles, he has made a decision to push through and keep pushing. Bob knows many people who have given up and accepted their fate as it is given to them.

Bob isn't like that. Now, he can't just lie down on the tracks and wait for that inevitable train to come along and take care of his misery.

Bob is a person of action now. He does it, even in the face of fear. He takes his rejection on the chin and risks more. He has become immune to it. He asks for the things that he wants, even if they tell him *NO*. He is done trying to please other people, and instead lives to make himself happy.

The more he succeeds at this, the more contagious his happiness becomes; he makes it his mission to share this with others. He isn't just making a difference in his own life—everyone around him who comes into contact with Bob wants a piece of what he has as well.

Bob focuses on his dreams and creates a plan—a strategy for getting there. Some people hate Bob; he doesn't do things the way they are supposed to be done, and he doesn't care much about fulfilling their expectations of him. He doesn't care for the haters of the world anymore; he doesn't listen to their opinions, whether good or bad. Bob is free. He still has fear, but it is a minute amount compared to the old Bob.

Now It's Your Turn...

Before we go any further, take thirty minutes to create your own "rejection-free persona" of the person you would like to be. This doesn't mean you have to change yourself in anyway. What we are doing is asking ourselves a question: "If I could act differently in a way that has a positive impact on my life, what would I do? How would I behave? What would I do differently?"

At this point, you may be asking, "Where do I begin? How do I start this journey to freedom? What is wrong with me, that I am so fearful?"

In my experience dealing with rejection issues and situations, I have come to **two conclusions**.

The first is that **we trap ourselves**. We pass judgments, formulate opinions, and fulfill expectations that lead to more of the same. When we buy into rejection, it solidifies the lies we formulated ages ago about our personal value and self-worth.

In a sense, we are all like Bob: **scared**. We are afraid of what the world is going to think; we are hesitant to put ourselves out there, because people will see us for the phony persona we have tried so hard to hide.

This is the foundation of self-rejection. We are harder on ourselves than anybody else. Staying hidden and out of sight is no way to live your life. It certainly isn't going to put you on the path to fulfilling your master goal or dream.

It is a continuous path to self-defeat. In our attempt to defuse rejection of ourselves, we just create more of what we fear.

How many times have you made a choice based on the desire to make someone else happy?

This is a failed system that just breeds unhappiness and an unfulfilled life. We do make choices—not for ourselves, but for our parents, lovers, partners, and employers. You might be saying, "As long as they are happy, I am happy." When others are happy, we feel good about that. But you need to take care of your own happiness, too.

Are you ready to make a choice?

Bob represents a level of freedom that is available to everyone. If someone disapproves of something he does because it disrupts their schedule, Bob can live with it just fine. Bob has everything he has ever wanted, and not because he had a great education or was popular. No, Bob has everything he wants because he knew what he wanted and created a clear plan for how he could get it. Bob set himself free by changing his attitude toward himself.

When you shift the attitude and thinking you have about who you are, you care less about what others are judging you for.

Bob made a decision that he would remove every obstacle between him and what he desired. Bob's plan didn't include working in an office all day for someone else, surrounded by people he disliked doing work he hated. Bob had bigger plans. Some people laughed at him. Some helped him.

The people who were there for Bob are his true friends. When you **choose your own** happiness above pleasing others just to gain approval, you see who your true friends are. Then, you can focus on pleasing the people in your life who care.

This isn't to say that we can just do whatever we want to do without consideration for others; it is about being who you want to be by choice, without the fear of being pushed aside or stepped on. When we experience rejection in all of its forms, in most cases we are rejecting ourselves before anyone else has a chance to.

This is about choosing the person you want to be, and not molding yourself into what others think you should be. All of us can have what we want if we can only muster the courage to break through the fear that holds us back from doing the things that we love.

This is the second realization: **You are what you decide to be at any given moment. You choose your actions, thoughts, and direction in life.**

Be prepared for resistance. This mindset goes against how others perceive you and want you to behave. To break free, you need to release yourself from others' expectations.

As we will see in a later chapter, asking for the things we really want is a powerful technique that can be mastered with practice. By asking, you open up the possibilities of what is available.

When you confront your fears and take action, amazing things start to happen. You will come to realize there is a major difference between living *in* fear and living *with* the fear. When we live in fear of being rejected, we develop an "escape-and-evade" attitude; it is easier to run from it than to face it head on.

The other option is to embrace what you are afraid of and develop a thick skin that can handle any kind of rejection. What we will learn to do is find that balance between conformity and delinquency.

One of the core lessons we are going to cover is that you can **choose yourself** above everything else.

How much are you going to sacrifice before you realize that when you accept any situation as something you have no control over, you give up that control and put yourself in a role of someone who is powerless?

The moment you decide that you have had enough of living in fear of being rejected, the changes in your life will begin.

This course is not a cure for rejection; it is a tool for dealing with it. You will always have situations and people who say *NO*. It is just a fact of life, no matter who you are.

What we are concerned with here is how you take the rejection. Will you crawl under a rock and never approach rejection again or will you take the rejection you experience and put it to good use?

"Effort only fully releases its reward after a person refuses to quit."

— Napoleon Hill

CHAPTER 3

Defeating Your Rejection Persona

"No one can make you feel inferior without your consent."

— Eleanor Roosevelt

I want you to consider the possibility that the rejection you have been experiencing has been largely a product of your own creation. By labeling ourselves as "rejected" or devaluing our own self-worth because of someone else's decision to NOT accept us, we are giving up our personal power to a large degree. In other words, you are allowing another to determine if you are good enough.

If you get turned down for whatever reason, it is because the timing just wasn't right. The person you asked didn't need your services at the time, or the situation wasn't working in favor of the other party because they have specific requirements that cannot be met by you at this time.

This is an opportunity in disguise. By being rejected, you can walk away with an opportunity to make yourself better for the next time around. Let's get out of the habit of looking at this as a failure or negatively thinking, "You see, I knew I was no good."

Now, imagine this scenario.

You are on your way to a job interview. As you walk into the building and are asked to take a seat, you notice the other applicants in the room. There are ten people, five women and five men. They are all decked out in new suits and are as professional as you've ever seen. Your mind immediately starts to undermine your confidence. You begin comparing yourself to these people and wondering if you should really be here.

Self-doubt begins to play with your mind. You begin to ask yourself questions that doubt your confidence:

"I don't have enough education or experience."

"These people are so much younger, refined and look more determined than me."

"What if I blow it? That will just prove I'm a failure."

"What if they ask me something and I freeze up?"

"What if it is a technical question, 'cause I'm really not good at tech stuff?"

"What was I thinking coming here in the first place?"

This is how the path to self-rejection begins. I know—this could happen to everyone. You get nervous and freeze up. You panic and have your moments of self-doubt. It is natural. For the self-rejection persona, it is a daily pattern of self-defeat. You kill your chances before you are given a chance to prove what you can do.

This is how you stay trapped—not by what the world is doing to you, but by what you are doing to yourself. When you can start to recognize the patterns of defeat and the negative thought process that starts tearing away at your confidence, then you can formulate a better plan to deal with it. When you recognize your role in this, you become the "director" of your choices instead of just an actor on stage.

One of the first steps in setting yourself free is to take responsibility for the rejection that you are creating without anyone else's help.

Scaling Up Responsibility

Every decision that you have made has brought you to this moment in your life. When you take responsibility for your current situation, just as it is, you become empowered by accepting your role in creating the situations you end up resenting. By recognizing that you do have control over your life and not everyone else, you move from a self-imposed victim state ("I have been rejected") to a state of deeper personal power ("Rejected? Me? Not so!").

The message that I am sharing with you in this book is:

> *The amount of fear you experience through rejection is in direct proportion to the power you give it. In doing so, you are giving people permission to reject you. This has nothing to do with the other side; it is your own choice. If you believe that your rejection is real, it is. This will repeat itself throughout your life as a destructive cycle.*

Two people can go through the same experience and feel completely different. One person accepts what happens as part of their growth and personal development; he or she has chosen himself or herself above the perceived rejection.

If you are not choosing your own life, you are rejecting it. If you reject it, you hand over the reins to those other people and let them make your choices for you. When you give up your right to live as a free individual, this is a form of self-rejection.

If living a life of feeling unworthy and inadequate is a prison, then liberating yourself by choosing who you are and how you want to live is the path to freedom. This is the aim: to choose yourself above all else and reject the limitations imposed by yourself.

You have to make clear-cut choices of which you want to be. If not, someone else will make those choices for you. If you don't make choices about your own life, rest assured someone else would make the choice for you. You can only be free when you exercise your right to be intentional about your actions.

It is a massive step when you can let go of self-judging condemnation. By silencing that inner critic that gets the "rejection" ball rolling, you can win the war instead of fighting your daily battles and exhausting yourself in the process.

If you are not responsible for your own life, then who is? If you cannot choose how you want to feel, and you have no control over your own feelings or emotions, then who does? If your emotions and thoughts are not being created and controlled by you, then who is the creator? By asking these questions, you will get the answers you seek.

It begins with taking responsibility for your life. I know this is a tall order. But playing the "victim" role and expecting someone else to carry you is not a healthy option—especially if your goal is to break the cycle of rejection.

Remember this: **You are not rejected unless you give others permission to do so.**

What I want you to consider is, how much of your rejection is actually you rejecting yourself? How much self-rejection are you going to take from your ego? What thoughts are you tuning into when this is going on? It's like the example I gave you for the job interview. You can be sitting alone in a quiet room with people around you and nobody engaging in conversation and suddenly your mind is having a two-way conversation with your fear.

You can control your thoughts. No one has a mind control device manipulating your thought patterns. So much of our suffering is self-inflicted. Responsibility isn't just a choice, but it is an intentional action. You take control the moment you recognize you have control.

Observe the communication you are having in your own mind. This is the "anonymous committee" that steps up when you are struggling with a situation and tries to give you advice.

When you reject that advice, it gets nasty and dishes out insults:

"You just don't have what it takes …"

"You got rejected because you have no skills …"

"If only you weren't so obese …"

"You see? I knew you'd screw up …"

"Why don't you quit while you're ahead?"

You've likely heard these voices before. They are your inner critics, the dark side of your past struggling to survive in a world you have never really learned to fit in to. When you reject yourself, you create a "tunnel-vision" mindset where every thought you create follows the direction of the one before it.

One put-down leads to another; each negative jab at your character folds into a more powerful punch. Your pattern of self-rejection escalates.

It is a chronic mental habit that fuels the deep convictions that:

- You aren't worth it.

- You don't matter.

- Your opinions and thoughts are useless.

- Nobody wants to know you.

- You should just give up now.

To free yourself, you have to take charge of the thoughts that are killing your spirit. Our bad thoughts that run amok are operating on autopilot; this means you can switch over and take full control of your flight path. If you question the reasoning behind these automatic and negative thoughts, you'll see that they are linked to your past programming. And that program can be overwritten and replaced by positive self-talk.

"Two men look out the same prison bars;

One sees mud and the other stars."

— Dale Carnegie, author of
How to Win Friends and Influence People

You can start this today, right now, by refusing to be a victim of rejection, by saying "No more!" to the ideas, beliefs, and thoughts that hold you prisoner and add to your fear. Be responsible and start to work on this now.

Putting a Stop to the Blame Game

We have a habit of blaming ourselves when things aren't right. When one of our parents criticized us, we blamed ourselves for not being good enough. When we were compared to others and told that we didn't measure up, we looked down on who we were. When we were made to feel unlovable by those closest to us, we believed that there was something wrong with us. The words hurt, and with it, that feeling of being abandoned, unwanted, and isolated.

If only I could be better or try harder.

If only I could do things as well as everyone else.

If only I were different somehow.

Years later, no matter how much we struggle to get past these negative feelings, they still stick. We have to make ourselves aware of what our emotions are trying to tell us. You have to question the feelings you have, especially when those feelings are hurting you.

Consider this question: "How can I choose myself when I have spent so many years rejecting who I am?"

When you get that rejection letter from the job you applied for, are they rejecting you? Or did someone else simply have a better skill set than you? How many other people were rejected for the same job?

When you ask someone out and they say no, are they rejecting you, or are you just not their type? Have you been rejected by every person you have ever approached?

When I analyzed all of the situations where I was afraid of being rejected, I came to a conclusion: When I thought it through rationally, I realized that people have preferences. I do not always fit with those preferences. There is no rejection here or anything to suspect. It is just the way it is.

When we are super sensitive about our issues with rejection, it feels as if everyone is out to reject us. In fact, it could be that they just desire something else at that time, and it could be that you don't fit those criteria. What we think is rejection is really a special form of "self-preference."

"Highly successful leaders ignore conventional wisdom and take chances. Their stories inevitably include a defining moment or key decision when they took a significant risk and thereby experienced a breakthrough."

— **Larry Osbourne**

CHAPTER 4

Self-Rejection and Those Old Voices

"The effects of rejection can either kill your muse or change your life."

— **Jane Champagne**

We often make choices that lead to mediocre results. Instead of choosing the things we really want, we settle for what is available. We also settle for what we believe we are worth, and for many people with rejection issues, that sense of worth isn't too high.

Instead of deciding what matters most to us, we decide to settle for what matters most to other people. Instead of rocking the boat and taking charge of our life, we drift and take life as it comes. And what we end up with is an outcome decided by someone else's needs instead of our own.

Before a job interview, I would come up with all of the reasons why they would probably refuse my application. I visualized myself failing and fumbling my words. I imagined the interviewer asking a question and my not having the answer. I doubted my skills and ability to clearly articulate my thoughts. I set myself up for falling before the fall.

How many times do you let yourself be rejected by your own hand before anyone else even has a crack at it?

It comes from accepting old beliefs that were recorded in our minds a long time ago. Being told that we were no good, being ignored or not chosen, being told *NO* because we just couldn't cut it or didn't have what it takes. The voices of the past, even though they are in the *distant* past, still have power over us.

You need to reclaim your power by making new choices that matter and that give you the upper hand in the game, instead of playing by their rules. These are the choices that empower your goals to take you from a position of powerlessness ("I'll settle for whatever you give me") to a position of power and choice ("This is what I want and I'll settle for nothing else").

You do this when you choose yourself first—in everything you do.

Rejection has taught us many things. It has taught us that self-doubt is first created from within. Others can doubt you (and they will), but it is *you* that doubts you the most.

Others can lack confidence in your abilities, but if you accept their perceptions as the only truth, you'll lose confidence in yourself. However, if you have already built up your confidence and you look at your life from a position of confidence, nobody can take that away from you.

A mentor of mine, who was an excellent salesman, once told me of these rejection seminars in his line of work that would toughen people up for getting told *NO*. He said that some salespeople couldn't get over the rejection that came with the job. They took it personally when a customer wouldn't buy, as if their sales tactics were faulty.

But the ones who made it would just say, "Okay, who's next?" The seminar would focus on the psychological impact of being rejected by customers. And breaking it down so that the sales people were not taking the *NO* personally. It is just a fact. No matter how good you are, there will always be someone who doesn't need what you are offering.

For every 100 sales refused, they would get 1 yes. People won't necessarily buy something from you because you are a nice person; they make purchases for their own reasons. If they say *NO*, it is most likely because they don't really need what you are offering.

But, nobody gets turned down forever. Eventually somebody will say *YES*, and then it becomes a numbers game. The salespeople who became frustrated and gave up after the first couple of weeks took it too personally, because they identified themselves as the cause for being told *NO*.

Life works in the same way. Some will say *YES* and some will say *NO*. You'll be accepted by some and rejected by many more. The people who free themselves from their habitual negative thinking can handle the judgments and words spoken by their critics. After all, who really has the power to judge and condemn?

Most people I meet think they are always right about their opinions. In almost every case, our judgments are misjudgments. When people judge you, do they really know who you are? Can they see inside your heart and make that observation with exact rectitude? Are they qualified to pass blame or to tear someone's reputation apart?

Hopefully, as we move deeper into this book, you can feel yourself opening up to the possibility that rejection is largely a state of mind. Better yet, when you come to accept that you are the one with your finger on the button of your life's changes, it becomes more about taking the initiative for and by yourself.

You have permission to put your self-worth first instead of believing you need approval for someone else. You have permission to hold yourself in the highest regard, without needing it to be validated by rewards or promotions. You can be yourself, without anyone telling you who you *should* be based on his or her own opinions.

"There comes a moment that defines winning from losing. The true warrior understands and seizes the moment by giving an effort so intensive and so intuitive that it could be called one from the heart."

— Pat Riley

CHAPTER 5

Redefining Your Personal Value

"After rejection – misery, then thoughts of revenge, and finally, oh well, another try elsewhere."

— Mason Cooley

My mentor asked me once, "If you were to place a value on your self-esteem, how much would it be?"

I didn't understand the question. How can you place a value on self-esteem? Or confidence? I was thinking in terms of dollars and cents and so, in a sarcastic attempt to be funny, I said, "A few dollars, I guess. Do you want to buy it?"

He said yes, took out his wallet and laid five bucks on the table. He wasn't joking either. He then said, "I just bought your self-esteem. Now how does it feel?"

My mentor always had a point to his lunacy, even if it came as "tough love" at times, but the lesson was solid:

- Your self-esteem has a value, just like your confidence.

- The amount of value is up to each of us, and nobody else.

Yet, can you remember a time when you accepted the minimum amount for something you held in high esteem? Maybe it was a yard sale and you'd just sold your favorite childhood toy for just a few bucks, because you really needed the money. You knew it was worth more, but you let it go anyway.

So, let me ask you this: How much are you worth? What is the price you place on your own value? How much is your time worth, or your best idea? These are things that have no price tag. You can choose the value of your importance, but nobody else can.

So why do people make choices that are really limitations in disguise?

We complain about our wages—but didn't you accept the job knowing how much it paid? We complain about having no time, and yet we spend hours a day watching TV. Isn't your time more valuable than watching TV instead of working on a project that has the potential to change your life? We complain about the people who drive us mad, but are we not choosing to have them in our lives?

When you decide to choose yourself, you make clear-cut choices about the course of action you are taking, even if that action is in doing nothing. When you meditate or think deeply about something, you're not moving your body very much, but these actions still add value to your life. When you play video games all day or surf junk sites on the Internet, you are engaging in another type of activity that is deciding what your future will look like.

By choosing your actions today, you are choosing how you will live your life tomorrow. By choosing the kind of person you want to be, you are *designing* your life instead of just letting it happen.

When you choose yourself above the rest, this elevates your confidence, eliminates fear and kicks your rejection issues right out the door. The choices in the *now* are the choices of all your *tomorrow*s combined.

We are so used to referring to the future as if it were something in the far-off distance, when in fact, it's the present moment and nothing more. This is all it ever has been.

You create your future through every choice you make in each present moment, which is the only place you really exist. Choose wisely how you will invest your time, emotional and physical energy. What do you want to learn? What courses can you take that will have a massive impact on your career and contributions? What can you participate in that is going to reduce your fear and make you more capable of taking positive action?

Choose your friends. Choose the people you want to spend time with. Who makes you feel so good that you want to spend all day or week with them? On the other hand, who doesn't make you feel this way? Is there anyone that holds you back or draws you into negative thinking?

We can't always choose the people we are surrounded by (for example, a co-worker that is in the same office as you, or a family member that you have friction with). We *can* choose how we will interact with them, and what role we play in that person's world.

You can choose your salary instead of allowing someone else to dictate how much you will be paid; you can choose the work you *want* to do instead of what you have to do for a paycheck. Did you choose your current job because you really wanted to do it, or are you just stuck there filling a chair? If so, why are you stuck? Did you make a choice to be stuck? Remember that you can choose all these things to make your life better, but by *not* choosing, you are also making another choice: **To accept everything as it is and do nothing to better your situation.**

Choosing yourself first is about making **steadfast choices.** It is the ultimate decision and a powerful choice you can make.

It is also not just a one-time thing. I have to constantly remind myself in any given situation that I am the one who makes the decisions.

Nobody else is going to give you a break. You can't rely on someone else to go easy on you just because you have sensitivity issues.

Remember Bob? He cares, but he only cares about the matters that are worth caring about.

If someone has an issue, it doesn't mean it has anything to do with you. Someone is in a bad mood? It's not your fault. Someone is unhappy with something you did and they blame you? Accept responsibility IF you believe it is warranted, but don't just assume that you're to blame.

People are often out of touch with their own reality and the scope of their emotions. They blame, scold, deny, judge, and move steadfastly toward a place of comfortable acceptance that makes them feel safe.

When you are critiqued or judged, it is natural to take it personally. Someone doesn't like your work, your style, your clothes, your character, and because of this, you think it is all you and that you need to change something to gain their approval.

You hear it all the time: *"If only they would be more like this, I'd be happier."*

If you had to change yourself every time someone offered an opinion or criticized you, you would be changing directions every ten minutes. Hold fast to your course: Stay true to who you want to be and not what you are being conned into believing you *should* be.

The Struggle with Self-Acceptance

Rejection always starts as an inside job. We will reject ourselves in 99% of the situations by deciding to not choose who we are. If you try to please everyone, you'll end up giving someone else all the leverage and the power to reject you further.

To some extent, we are all a little self-conscious of what everyone thinks of us. We place a value on an opinion even if it isn't always accurate. You might agree to something just to avoid a look of disapproval or letting someone down, even if it means agreeing to something you didn't want in the first place.

We try hard to be liked, to be accepted, and to be loved. By acting in a way that people approve of, they'll think more highly of us, we think. They'll invite us into their circle—until they figure out that we have been faking it, and then we get ousted out again.

My greatest fear, when I would meet someone new, was: *"What if this person doesn't like me? What if they discover how weird or awkward or uncomfortable I am around people?"*

Everybody has different tastes, needs, and wants. As hard as it is to accept, not everybody wants what you have to give. At times they will reject your skills ("You just don't have the skills for this job") or they will reject your love ("Sorry, you're not my type; I like short, stocky men"). They either want something else or someone else. It is just a fact of life: we are selective creatures and make choices based on our own needs.

What you perceive as rejection is really someone making choices based on their needs at that time. If you struggle with hypersensitivity, every form of rejection becomes a personal barrier. You think it is you, when in fact, it is really the other person or the situation that is driving their choices at the time.

Because someone convinced you in your childhood days that you were not worthy, those negative emotions and feelings and that hurt are still there. When you were criticized, you tried harder to please someone—a parent, a teacher, or someone close. But the criticism continued.

Someone took your confidence away, and now you want it back. This experience has created a condition of hypersensitivity. When you are in a situation that challenges your self-esteem, you become extra sensitive once that fear is tapped into.

Challenge Your Inner Skeptic

The skeptics and critics will always be around. They have nothing to do but target others who are trying to do something positive with their lives. They only have a say in what constitutes your personal worth if you give them that permission, but you don't have to do that. You can keep it.

You can decide. **Set aside and schedule time out during the day** to really reflect on the emotions you are experiencing.

Stay in touch with the emotions, thoughts, and feelings that you are experiencing in any given moment. Tapping into your fear will indicate what needs to be approached and handled. If you are procrastinating or resisting taking action, underneath that fear you are practicing "rejection avoidance." This keeps the problem buried, but not solved.

Take time each day to observe your emotions. How are you feeling? What are you feeling? What do you feel anxious about? What can you do right now to face this situation? Writing your feelings down is an excellent way to bring them to your conscious awareness. Just try beginning each writing attempt with the words *"I feel …"* and then write whatever comes to mind at that time. Write until you feel you have expressed everything you are feeling.

By putting yourself out there and challenging your fears of rejection, you are opening the floodgates to *real personal empowerment*.

People with a rejection persona think they must be loved by all or hated by everyone. But the reality is, nobody is either loved or hated by everyone. It's not that cut and dry. You try to find acceptance in everyone and sooner or later you'll break your own value systems just to earn that acceptance.

Action Plan

In its negative mode, self-talk is like having someone stand behind you and drill you on all the things you do wrong. The inner critic is a harsh teacher. What is worse is that we pass these negative thoughts on to our children and share our negativity with those around us.

Listen to your self-talker when you are alone. What are you saying to yourself? Do you use negative and demeaning put-downs? The person who is aware of and can direct their self-talk has the rejection habit licked, and this will have a big impact on their life.

"All forms of self-defeating behavior are unseen and unconscious, which is why their existence is denied."

— **Vernon Howard**

CHAPTER 6

Breaking Free of the Predictable Path

"No matter what challenges you are faced with, or the opinions people have of you, rejection in and of itself from others is not a valid system to predict your future."

— Anonymous

When you avoid being rejected, you eliminate all possibilities of losing, looking bad, or failing completely. You play it safe. You look for the non-fail, safe methods that are guaranteed to reduce your failure rate. Unfortunately, this path reduces your success rate also. This is the path of *predictability*.

Predictability works one of two ways: you either have a guarantee that it will work out in your favor with a positive outcome, or you avoid the situation completely for fear of failing or losing something valuable.

Relying on predictability as a course of action creates a coping mechanism for passive-aggressively dealing with your deeper, unresolved issues.

The questions to ask yourself are as follows:

"What am I protecting?"

"What am I in fear of losing?"

"What do I risk not gaining if I avoid taking any chances at all?"

But the danger of creating a predictable life is that you favor routine over change; although routine serves us well in many ways, if you use it to avoid changing as a means of escape, you are not moving toward freedom but are building larger walls to fortify your personal prison. You are not really free until you can confront the fear of making real choices.

Do you know what happens when life is built on predictable choices? You avoid the difficulties and struggles that others face, in order to eliminate the chances of failing. While this might eliminate your risk factor, by not taking any form of risk and not doing what your heart really wants you end up feeding into your rejection even more. You make it stronger. It prospers, and you fall deeper into the rabbit hole that you have tried desperately to escape from.

Rejectionism is more than just a condition; it becomes a way of life. This way of life chooses the back-end road. You avoid plateaus that lead to higher levels of growth. When life becomes a narrow highway, you make predictable choices that lead to obvious outcomes.

Here is how you create a life of predictability that keeps you trapped:

- You avoid talking about an issue with your spouse or partner for fear that they will not understand you; so instead you complain about the situation to a friend

- You ask for $5 instead of $500 because you know that there is a much better chance of getting less money

- You ask for a date with someone that is an easy catch because the person you really want is out of your league; meanwhile, you fantasize about what it would be like to be with the person you really like;

- You don't try to change your current bad habits even though they are destructive and unproductive; you end up doing the same things repeatedly because there is safety in what you know, even if it doesn't work very well

- You stay in the same job you hate because they all know you and it's a steady paycheck; taking another job and starting over is risky if it doesn't work out

- You don't make any new friends because you prefer the company of old friends that already know you.

It comes down to **risk**. When you make choices based on the risk factor, what you are doing is setting yourself up for success by getting what you are asking for, but not what you really want.

This is what Steve Jobs meant when he said, "Don't settle."

Predictability is about taking second best. You ask for what you can get and not what you really value. Driven by feelings of shame and low self-esteem, living a predictable lifestyle almost guarantees your success.

Make your own list of how you sustain a predictable lifestyle that is actually keeping you trapped.

Now I am not suggesting being predictable is a *bad* thing, because it isn't. But if it is what you do to stay where you are for fear of moving forward, you are doing yourself a huge disservice. Just think of all the opportunities you are missing out on. The experiences you could be having now if you do what you're scared to do. The people you could connect with and places you could go.

I stayed in the same job for fifteen years because I was terrified of applying for a new position. What if I didn't get the job? What if they questioned my education? What if I didn't have the skills or lacked something they needed?

I stayed stuck in relationships I resented and eventually hated because of my fear. I made excuses.

"Oh, we've been together for a long time. It's too late to find someone else."

I avoided large crowds and groups. I hated social functions. People talk about themselves and their accomplishments—I had none to think of. I took no risks and consequently had nothing to brag about. I didn't want people questioning my background or finding out the truth, that I was just ordinary, with no Master's degree or awards to speak of.

I rarely made new friends. I stayed with the same people. It was more predictable that way, and therefore safer. I am not saying there is anything wrong with having the same friends throughout your life—of course not. But are you trying to meet new people? Do you fear social situations because of what they might say or do?

Our choices become pathways that support our rejectionism through controlling the outcome. There is little risk. Life is boring, but it's safe. We don't have to face the shame or humiliation that comes with being rejected.

What is the solution? How do you break out of this life of predictability in order to start living? How is it going to feel if at the end of your life you look back and see all the chances you gave up because you were afraid?

Breaking Your Predictable Pathways

We choose the people, places, and situations that have the least chance to reject us.

It could be an old relationship or a job you've been in for the past twenty years. You might not favor your current situation, but you'll stick with it to avoid changing. Be honest—change requires courage. It takes discipline to find this courage at times.

Being predictable is all about avoiding change; and avoiding change is strongly associated with avoiding rejection. One of the key reasons that we never get beyond rejected child syndrome is because we spend most of our lives hiding from it.

You can't recover if you are constantly on the run.

So, the question you need to ask yourself is this:

"What do I have to lose?"

In order to break your predictability, you have to do the things that you would normally not do. These are easy to identify. They are the actions that, inwardly, you have always wanted to try but externally you haven't, because of the negative outcome you've already visualized taking place. In other words, you won't because you're not willing to gamble with your humiliation or shame. Your rejection.

But *you can do this*. What is the worst that can happen?

You can break out of the predictable patterns that keep you stuck.

Breaking Predictability

Now, here are two steps to breaking predictability and putting yourself out there:

Step 1: Take note of your daily habits.

I did this step for a six-month period where I would record my activities every day. This included not only the tasks I did but also the people I associated with, the places I would frequent, and even the food I ate. I discovered that my routine was the same every day. I even took the same route home every night.

By breaking up your routine, just making small changes here and there, you can begin to put some uniqueness back into your lifestyle. When this happens, it expands your risk scale and you'll be ready to try new things.

Why does this matter? You'll get comfortable with risk-taking, and when I say taking risks, I'm not talking about jumping between buildings, but realistic risks. Like meeting new people. Putting your voice out there. Defeating the fear of being judged or criticized.

Then try new things. Go to a different coffee shop where different people hang out. Get out of your familiar zone and into something new. It's natural to have a routine that we are used to, but is your routine keeping you stuck in one place? I realized it was and I wanted to make a few changes that got me trying new stuff.

Step 2: Put yourself in a situation that gets you rejected.

I had a job interview some time ago. It went well even though I didn't end up getting the position. But I knew I wasn't going to get it anyway. I did it on purpose because I wanted to desensitize my fear of interviews. I have never been good at interviewing, so I put myself into a position where I knew I'd be turned down.

It worked. After several more interviews, I didn't care what they thought. I wasn't good enough for their corporation? There were plenty of other opportunities. I was going to look for them and take advantage of everything I could. The funny thing is, the one company I didn't think would hire me actually made me the offer. I didn't take the job, but I am pretty sure that the reason they offered me the position was because during the interview I was relaxed and confident. Sometimes, just not giving a hoot pays off.

When you do something that you usually wouldn't do, you are stepping out of your predictable comfort zone. Everyone has a comfort zone in which they feel totally safe. It's like a protective cocoon. We need this for stability and to feel safe. But if your comfort zone is designed in such a way that it becomes a prison, consider changing up old habits. This doesn't have to be an all-or-nothing maneuver. Taking one solitary action—even a small step—can create a multitude of waves.

Action Plan

Think back to a time in your life when you took a risk on something and failed. Maybe you tried a new line of work or invested in something that lost you money. You asked someone out and they said *NO*. You asked for money but it was only a fraction of what you really wanted. You passed on a business strategy because you feared it wouldn't work out.

Put yourself in this position again and visualize what you would do differently now, if given another chance. How would you talk to the person you are interested in getting to know? How much money would you ask for, and how would you ask for it? What job would you show up to for an interview, knowing full well that you are the person for it?

In order to break out of your comfort trap, visualize it happening. You have to see yourself doing it. Run the scenario through your mind over and over again. Every time you do, you make the vision stronger.

Visually and mentally see yourself taking the actions that you really want to take. Try this for ten minutes a day. Spend time in the morning visualizing how your day is going to go when you do the things that are outside your comfort zone. You will start to break the predictability trap and move closer to setting yourself free.

"You can search throughout the entire universe for someone who is more deserving of your love and affection than you are yourself, and that person is not to be found anywhere. You yourself, as much as anybody in the entire universe, deserve your love and affection."

— Buddha

CHAPTER 7

Rejection and Love Dependency

"Remember that the best relationship is one in which your love for each other exceeds your need for each other."

— Dalai Lama

After spending most of our lives feeling unloved, ashamed, or humiliated, many of us have internalized the core belief that nobody can possibly love us. We are convinced that we are destined to be alone, and that being alone is better than being rejected.

But when this happens, your love for others becomes clingy, desperate, and eventually hurtful. Love becomes conditional instead of unconditional. You start to love for survival instead of developing healthy relationships.

This fuels the belief that, because you are unlovable, those that are closest to you will inevitably reject you. This in turn lends itself to love addiction or love desperation: when you are so desperate for people to like you, it repels people away.

You either try too hard to get others to accept you, appearing needy and desperate, or you hold yourself back, terrified to put yourself out there on the chance that your love will be thrown back at you. By putting yourself out there, telling people you care is like walking on a ledge afraid of falling off.

Going through rejection in relationships is a major trap for those with a rejection persona. You never really feel accepted or that your love is valued. Criticism and shame are at the front of every interaction.

Our relationships are based largely on trying to hide this rejection. But the more intimate a relationship becomes, the more impossible it is to put up a fake front. As soon as the other person realizes how desperate you are, or that you are not being totally transparent, the relationship ends.

The cycle then repeats itself in the next one. Vulnerability is not an emotion most of us are willing to put at risk, so we hide who we are from the people we want to love the most. In the end it is a lose-lose situation.

In the relationship where rejection is an issue, love is something that is based on conditions. You are lovable if you are good; you are lovable if you follow the rules and do as you are told. You are lovable if you don't embarrass me at the party.

This reinforces the belief you formed in childhood that if you do as we say, you will be loved. Conditional love is always built on a foundation of conditions or requirements that must be met before you receive the love you so desperately crave. This stems from a critical parent or guardian when you were growing up.

Nothing you did was ever good enough, so you tried harder. When it seemed that absolutely nothing was good enough, you gave up and gave into the feeling of being defective. This is one of the origins of developing a rejection persona.

First of all, **conditional love isn't real love**. This kind of love falls under the pretense that "I'll love you IF you ..."

To become worthy of another person's approval, you have to earn it somehow. It is like going to work and getting paid a salary. We will pay you this much IF you do the job we expect. **Love isn't a condition**. It is an absolute. It has to be, or else it becomes a negotiation.

If you have children, then you know what this means. You love your children without conditions. Yes, they misbehave and act up and do the things you don't want them to do. They might even get into real trouble someday. But they are still your kids. Unconditional.

Now, in your daily life, most people you associate with are not going to love you unconditionally. You will be met with conditions in most situations in your life. People will like you if you do this or that; you do a good job for your manager, you're on her good side; you screw up, you're on her other side.

The rejection persona has become accustomed to this conditioned way of love. However, many people who crave love crave unconditional love. But because you are conditioned, you try to meet all the conditions that everyone places on you in hopes you fulfill another person's wishes and receive that unconditional acceptance you're seeking. It's a vicious cycle.

We spend most of our lives "seeking," searching for the things that are missing on the inside. We missed out on love when we were kids, and now we want someone else to give it to us. Our parents didn't give us the love we should have received, and now there is a big hole in our lives where love should be.

The dilemma is, you'll spend the rest of your life trying to fill that big hole if you are searching for it "out there." The external world cannot give you anything that is lasting or permanent.

You were never accepted or recognized for anything of value, so you feel worthless. The result: you seek acceptance and worth from others. And how much do you need before you can feel totally fulfilled? It's like a bottomless pit, and there is no amount of encouragement or positive reinforcement that anybody can give you that would ever be good enough.

When you spend your life seeking and expecting some form of payback, you want what is owed to you: love, love, and more love. As a child you were devalued and underappreciated. School marks were never good enough, you were poor at sports, or at home you always seemed to be "in the way."

It is painful to accept, but if you do the deep analysis work and come to terms with your rejection persona in relationships, you will reach this conclusion: The love you are trying to find and extract from your relationships will never be enough. It isn't the same thing, not the way your parents could have given it to you. You will only become frustrated and start rejecting your partner or putting them down as a means to defend your position in the relationship. Power struggles will then erupt and the relationship will take a bad turn.

Rejectees struggle with unconditional love most of their lives. If you didn't receive it when you were a child, you'll spend the rest of your life trying to get it from the people who may be unwilling or incapable of giving it to you.

This puts a lot of pressure on the person you have only been dating for a few weeks, and you want to be loved like nobody else has ever loved you before. When that person rejects your demands, you become needy and desperate. Picking up on that hungry dependence, the other person will flee the relationship.

People who have dependency issues are looking for unconditional love in all the wrong places. We've established that. So, the question becomes this:

"Where do I find this unconditional love?"

Just as you have to **choose yourself first**, so you can build trust, reliability, and confidence, and so do you have to **love yourself first**. Asking the world to give you this love is unrealistic. You will fail in holding these expectations for others.

Of course, we all need and desire love from other people, but depending on any one person completely to fill in that missing part of your life will lead to an emotional setback and eventually disappointment. But when we treat people we come into contact with each day with respect, admiration and appreciation, they will pick up on your positive attitude towards them.

As the **Dalai Lama** wisely expressed: *"If you want others to be happy, practice compassion. If you want to be happy, practice compassion."*

I have found no greater way to create unconditional love than to give away the best of myself at any given time. I know this sounds like a tall order, and it isn't always easy to just accept everyone, but try to open up your mind and heart as much as you can. Instead of desperately seeking that love you feel is missing, turn it around and realize that you have all that you need: It just has to be nurtured.

The one obstacle that holds people back is putting themselves in a position where they are vulnerable. We are afraid to just put ourselves out there in case we get injured or taken advantage of. But protecting ourselves is what we have been doing for a long time, and even though it feels natural and necessary to stray away from that rejection, by letting go of that fear of vulnerability, you are reducing the pain of going through a rejection.

How to Practice Unconditional Love

You want to experience unconditional love? Treat people without conditions. Do things for them without expecting anything. Say nice things about them and don't ask for anything in return. The moment you do something for someone and you attach a want or expectation to it, you are building that disappointment up again. Successful relationships are based on four important values:

- Mutual respect

- Valuing the people you are with

- Avoiding any form of harsh criticism

- Giving without heavy expectations

Relationships that are based on a give-and-take strategy don't experience the unconditional love that could be fostered if practicing these four simple principles. But the "I'll love you if you love me"—in any relationship, not just romantic—sets you up for failure.

As soon as one person decides that they're not sharing that love anymore, it's gone. Your unconditional-love pact has ended. You must wake up to this truth if you are going to get over this massive hurdle. It is time to accept that the unconditional love that you should have had as a kid most likely isn't going to happen.

One lesson I learned from having been through several dependency-type relationships is this: You can't get something from someone if they aren't willing or capable of sharing. Nobody can give you what he or she doesn't have. And the fact is, relying on someone to fulfill all of your needs isn't going to work out in the end.

If you have really deep issues around codependency, you might need a big push to get yourself to take action. You'll only be lovable when you can learn to give it away.

The cure isn't complicated—look at how you interact in relationships and take a moment to tap into your feelings. Are you being genuine, or putting up a front? Are you being completely open, or do you feel that you're hiding your true self for fear of being exposed? Are you interested in this relationship because of its potential, or is there an underlying motive?

Unconditional love is getting to that place where you can accept yourself completely, without illusions of perfectionism or feeding into the needy wants of a childhood ego. Unconditional love isn't what you have to have for everyone, but it is what you need for yourself and your children.

Many of our rejection-persona issues stem from childhood. They started there, and it is too late to go back and fix what was done. But you can start moving forward today.

Focus on loving yourself in a way that you never were as a child. Revisit your childhood and re-experience those feelings of shame, guilt, and rejection. Reach out to yourself and give the love that was withheld. Visualize yourself wanting these things as a child and not getting them. Walk yourself through the pain of those moments. Pull yourself back in if you try to escape. Stay focused on that memory and let it happen. See yourself wanting that approval and getting rejected for it.

Tapping into these memories brings up painful emotions. But these are the feelings that you have been escaping from most of your life. By avoiding what happened, you are keeping the lies that built this false persona. Exposing the truth and fully realizing that it was not your fault frees you from this pain over time.

Action Plan

Look for areas in your life where you expect love but you aren't getting it. Is it from your wife, husband, partner, or lover? How about your children? Do you have unrealistic demands? Are you needy or do you come across as demanding for love?

Focus on giving your love to someone in a way that you never received it. By this I don't mean romantic love, but genuine caring for other people. Because rejection is such a deep and painful issue, most people don't want to admit or even recognize that they have these issues. But you do. Everyone does to some extent, some more than others.

By helping others, you will create the opportunity to increase your personal value. I have found that by helping people, I naturally developed a deeper love for myself that was never there before. Trust me, if you like and respect yourself, you'll never have to worry about lack of love in your life.

If there is anything that can remove that fear of rejection, it is putting yourself out there, loving yourself more, and genuinely embracing the kindness of others. A lot of people out there need people like you. Don't let that "rejection bug" stop you from giving it.

Make a list of the things you feel ashamed or embarrassed about.

Is it...

- Being alone?

- Feeling jealous or envious of others?

- Wanting to be someone else instead of who you could be?

Take yourself through your emotions and observe how you are feeling. When we can identify the situations that trigger rejection, it puts us in a better position to take action. By knowing when you are experiencing a "rejection moment," you can put an end to that vicious cycle.

PART 2:
Just Ask for It!

CHAPTER 8

Why We Fear Asking

"Rejection doesn't have to mean you aren't good enough; it often just means the other person failed to notice what you have to offer."

— Ash Sweeney

Asking for the things we want the most is one of the hardest things to do. We fear hearing that *NO* word more than any other word in the language.

Think back to when you were a kid. Chances are you asked for everything you could. When you didn't get it you became persistent and demanded it. If your parents said no (which they often did) you'd go away for a while but return later with a new plan of attack. You probably resorted to negotiating— "I'll clean my room for a week if you let me have what I want."

Eventually you either got what you wanted or you finally conceded that you had lost. You would pursue every avenue until what you wanted—that new toy or the latest cool gadget—was yours.

But over the years we change.

We start asking for less and end up taking what is available. We lose that hardline negotiating and whining that worked as kids. Our parents often told us to stop whining or being selfish, so we did. After all, nobody wants to be labeled as selfish.

This brings us to the **power of asking,** one of the core themes in this book, and a primary obstacle when it comes to facing rejection.

The fear of being rejected is what stops a rejectee from taking any kind of action. Instead of demanding or even asking, we lean toward acceptance and passive numbness. This is a path that leads to suffering. We suffer when we go without while watching others get what they want because they asked for it. You might develop resentment, not only towards those people who are "braver" than you but you'll label yourself as weak and a coward.

When you have to go without because you can't muster up the courage to ask for it—when we go without the things we crave, knowing that we could have them if we only stood up and did something—it hurts. We are buying into our own rejection and, in fact, creating more of it. You might avoid conflict or rejection by not asking, thinking you were spared the emotional pain of hearing *NO*, but the consequences of this are far worse in the long run.

In their groundbreaking and bestselling book, *The Aladdin Factor*, authors **Jack Canfield** and **Mark Victor Hansen** (*Chicken Soup for the Soul*) tell us that nothing comes without first making the decision that you deserve it, you want it, and you are going to have it. Then, knowing these facts, you seek out the right people who are going to help you to get it.

In this section, that is exactly what we are going to discuss: how to make a decision based on what you want, then figure out your plan for getting it.

Asking for the things that you want is one of the best strategies and habits for developing personal freedom. When you take a risk by asking for something, you open up huge doors for yourself. Opportunity doesn't come knocking and looking for takers; we have to forge the opportunity by stepping up, saying *YES*, and taking direct action. **Asking is the key to taking charge of your life**, and to the resulting success that follows.

The bottom line: **If you fail to ask, you fail to get.**

Here are some reasons we don't ask:

1. The answer will be a definite *NO* (so why bother).

2. You will be embarrassed or humiliated if rejected.

3. You fear that if they say *YES*, you'll be expected to return the favor.

4. We undermine our own confidence, believing that we are not worthy to receive this.

5. Pride gets in the way when we associate asking with begging.

6. Low self-esteem issues: my needs are not that important and I can do without.

7. I might be judged for being poor for not having this already.

When you ask for something that you want, your confidence skyrockets and you prove to yourself that the fear you had was just an illusion keeping you trapped.

When you ask, you are desensitizing your fear of rejection. We will discuss desensitization more in the next section but, for now, know that developing the *asking habit* is the key to eliminating rejection fears.

For years I was too passive. I expected everything to just come my way, or that people would figure out what I wanted and give it to me without my asking.

But nobody knows better than you do what you want. People cannot read your mind. If you wait for someone to figure out what you want, and then hope they give it to you, you could be in for a long wait and a big setup for disappointment. This isn't patience; it is a form of self-denial.

If you knew all you had to do was ask, you could have everything you've ever wanted. But many people don't have what they want and they go without because they haven't asked for it.

Why? We believe that the answer will be *NO*. And hearing that word—*NO*—traces right back to childhood when we were denied the things we really wanted. Who denied us? Parents, teachers, and peers.

How many times have you been told, "Don't ask for it, because you're not getting it"? Fair enough—but regardless, we didn't get it; the want is still there. I can still recall things I wanted in my childhood and never got. Can you?

This sounds like such a simple concept. You ask for things all the time, right? But it's not the frequency of asking that matters. You have to ask for the right things.

If you ask for the wrong things all your life, any request will do. Why ask for oranges if you want apples? In other words, stop asking for the things you don't want or need.

There are three truths about asking:

1. People who ask for what they want usually get rejected.

2. People who don't ask for what they want never get rejected because they never ask.

3. People who keep asking for what they want may get rejected, but eventually they'll get what they want.

I came to the conclusion that, I could keep getting what I have always gotten. Or I could push myself to try and get the stuff I never imagined getting. When you ask for what you want and not what you think you're worth, it is like putting the key into the right door lock: You open up a whole new world of possibilities.

It follows a simple principal:

*   Ask and you may receive.

*   Don't ask and you'll never receive.

When I started asking for things, it all changed. I got some *NO*s; but I also got some people who said *YES*. And my averages were good. I received a *YES* about 60% of the time. If I hadn't asked for anything, I'd have gotten nothing. 60% works better than 0%.

Asking is paramount to succeeding. This is especially true when it comes to asking for help. I'll talk more on this later.

For years, I lived in hesitation because I feared the answer would confirm what I already believed: I wasn't worth it, and that's why I was constantly rejected.

This "asking action" changed the way I think about how to overcome my rejection addiction. Most of my life I shied away from asking for anything. I didn't want to get in the way or bother anyone. In other words, I didn't want to put myself in a position where I risked being rejected. If they said *NO*— and that was a very good possibility—it would reinforce every belief I had about myself that I was unworthy of getting the things I really wanted.

How will you know that you can have something if you never ask for it? By asking for what you want, you boost your chances of receiving this exponentially. If you don't ask for it, your chances of getting nothing would be almost guaranteed. Nobody is going to read your mind; they don't know what you want, and even if they did, would they just offer it to you? Most likely not.

Years ago, I stopped asking for what I wanted out of fear that I would leave myself open to vulnerability, I would owe somebody something that I could never repay, or they would see me as weak or needy. My pride would get in the way.

> *There are so many things that I have wanted in my life that I never received for one reason only. It wasn't lack of money or skill; it was the absence of courage to ask for what I desired most.*

Not asking for what you want because of the fear of looking stupid, feeling powerless, being humiliated—those are all fears of rejection. You learned at a young age that is it better to just take what you can get instead of risking everything by asking for what you want. You don't want to appear needy or helpless.

There is a price to pay for not asking. You might avoid the humiliation of being rejected, but by avoiding asking for the stuff you really want, you will lose a lot more. By trading in your pride and fear of embarrassment, you could be giving up large sums of money (asking for a raise), your freedom (asking for time off), and the opportunity to thrive instead of survive.

Here is a list of reasons why asking counts:

- If you don't ask for directions, you end up going the wrong way

- If you don't ask for financial assistance to go back to school, you can't get a good education and you end up unemployed, possibly permanently

- If you don't ask to borrow someone's car because yours broke down and you need to get to work, you miss a day's pay and the manager is not happy

- If you don't ask that person out on a date, someone else will

- If you don't ask for more money in your work, you'll have less money

- If you don't ask for support, you end up doing it alone

- If you don't ask how it's done, you'll end up doing it the wrong way

- If you don't ask for an extension on that deadline, you'll be up late tonight trying to get it all done

- If you don't ask for time off, you work harder and risk burning out

- If you don't ask the waiter to heat up your dinner more because you want it hotter, you end up paying full price for an expensive meal that's cold

- If you don't ask your spouse to listen to you when you have something important to say, then you end up unfulfilled, unhappy, and resentful

- If you don't ask for a second chance, you have to accept your first attempt as a painful lesson in failing

By not asking, you are taking a big risk. You are making a decision to be less, have less, and ultimately to want less. You will eventually make excuses for yourself and say, "Oh that's okay, I didn't really need it anyway."

Really? You don't want help with something? You don't want more money for your hard work or more time off? You don't want more friends or people who will listen to you? You don't want more confidence? You don't want a discount on your hotel room? You don't want to go out with that girl that lives down the street, even though she's been looking at you every morning as you jogged by? You don't want a bank loan to buy a new house?

I don't believe it.

And neither should you.

Selling yourself short is telling the world "I'm not worthy of any of these things, so I won't ask for anything." If that's the case, you'll end up shorthanded and short changed. You'll get what others give you. And what they give you could be the remains of the good stuff they are finished with.

*When you don't ask for the things that you truly
desire, there is always somebody else that will.
While you are busy waiting for someone to give you
what you secretly want, others are pushing ahead,
asking, and receiving their gifts.*

The Risk Worth Taking

If you could ask for what you wanted from this day on, where would you start? What would you ask for first?

Make a list of all the stuff you have been holding out on. Would you ask for help with a project? Would you approach the bank and apply for a loan so you can start that business? Would you ask for better benefits at work? Would you reach out to your friend for help, or a stranger?

Make a list of all the things that would improve your situation drastically. Here are some ideas:

- What would you ask for at home?

- What about when you go out in public? Would you ask someone to move their car so you could squeeze into the next parking spot?

- What would you ask for at a restaurant? A café? A shopping mall?

- Would you ask for a price reduction on older items in a shop?

- Would you ask a stranger to have coffee?

- Would you ask someone to loan you money on the promise that you would return it within a specified time frame?

- Would you ask someone to treat you with more respect and stop criticizing?

The power of asking is one of the key components to really kicking your fear of rejection out of your life. You can numb your fear by taking action and doing something every day that desensitizes you to this fear.

Asking is equated to taking risk. But it is **a good risk**. It's the risk that gets you out of a rut and puts you in greater control of your life. You feel powerful and centered. By asking, you are taking charge of your life. That fear of being rejected is reduced to a minuscule whimper. Eventually you won't even feel it anymore.

Now that is something worth having.

If it is true that, by asking, you get what you ask for, you also deprive yourself of the things you don't ask for.

Don't ask and you won't get; ask once and you might get it. Ask again and again and you'll increase your chances of getting anything exponentially!

That's how simple it is.

At the very least, by asking for what you want and putting yourself out there, you'll build up a tough resistance to hearing *NO*. The more you hear *NO*, the easier it becomes. You will desensitize yourself to being told to bugger off.

"Recognizing that you are not where you want to be is a starting point to begin changing your life."

— Deborah Day

When you ask and someone looks at you with doubt and you know they won't comply with your request, instead of feeling that pang of anxiety that says "Ouch, I've been told *NO* again," you'll develop a tougher skin for getting told *NO*. Instead of fearing rejection, you will come to embrace you.

In his bestselling novel *Rejection Proof,* author **Jia Jiang** put rejection to the test. For one hundred days he put himself in situations where he asked for literally anything, often very absurd stuff that people would certainly say *NO* to. Several times he was shocked that he actually got a *YES* and was given the opportunity to try something he normally would never have thought of.

By putting himself in situations in which he was almost guaranteed to fail, he desensitized himself to getting told *NO*. After one hundred days he had more freedom than he had ever experienced.

As Jiang experienced through this experiment, you won't be cured by getting rejected once, but by doing it continuously. It acts as a major boost of confidence and pushes the power of rejection right out the door. We will discuss this more in section 3, but as the experiments in rejection have proven, you only earn your freedom and break those "chains" when you get out there and do it.

For years, I asked for nothing unless I absolutely had to. If it was something I needed and couldn't do without, and I was in a position where asking another human being was the only way, I'd do it. But only in extreme circumstances. I was like a silent watchdog that always had my eye on things I desired but stayed in the shadows and watched, while others moved ahead by taking action.

For years I made excuses for not asking. I would say things like ...

"I can figure it out for myself."

"Oh no, don't trouble yourself. I'll take care of it."

"It's not important."

"I'll ask tomorrow."

If this is you, let's take action to change this. Don't be a silent watchdog and suffer without. You deserve to have everything you have ever wanted. You deserve it no matter what your mind tells you.

"One of life's fundamental truths states, "Ask and you shall receive." As kids we get used to asking for things, but somehow, we lose this ability in adulthood. We come up with all sorts of excuses and reasons to avoid any possibility of criticism or rejection."

— **Jack Canfield**, author of
The Aladdin Factor

CHAPTER 9

Essentials to Asking for What You Want

"Everyone at some point in life have faced rejection and failure, it is part of the process to self-realization."

— **Lailah Gifty Akita**

Here are the eight steps you can use for asking for anything you want. This will be hard in the beginning, but after putting yourself out there and doing it, you'll get the hang of it. Soon you'll be asking for everything without second guessing yourself.

The 8 Steps to Getting to YES

Step 1: STOP thinking about the negative outcome, which is getting rejected and hearing *NO*. It doesn't matter, because if you don't ask, you're rejecting yourself and you won't get anything anyway. You have created a lose-lose situation before you've begun. Focusing on a bad outcome is going to affect the way you ask, if you do at all.

By expecting to be refused, you'll go into the situation lacking any confidence at all. People are much more apt to give you something if you act like you really deserve it. If you show fear or you are already dreading that first *NO*, it will show. If you are focused on the outcome not turning out the way you want it to, turn it around so that you visualize yourself getting that *YES*.

Step 2: Visualize the action of ASK, not the response—it is not important that you get a *YES*. Of course, that is what you want, but if you bank everything on getting that *YES* and you keep getting told *NO*, you'll revert back to thinking about the negative outcome.

The positive outcome is the action of you asking. Not the result. You have been so focused on the response that you forget it is the courage that we had to conjure up to ask in the first place that is the real victory. Forget about the outcome. Focus on the action of asking. You can do this by **visualizing** yourself doing it.

See yourself opening that door and walking into a room. The person that stands between you and what you desire is sitting there in a chair in the center of that room. Imagine walking right up to him or her and asking for that one thing you have always wanted. Now, take it a step further and see them reacting to your request.

You can run through various outcomes; would they get angry and start shouting, or smile and just say, "Sure, you can have that. Why didn't you ask me sooner?" I used this technique a lot when I struggled with asking. I still do. Visualizing yourself doing it is a powerful approach to psyching up your courage, and it actually gets you excited about doing this. You'll be less fearful and anxious.

Step 3: Ask yourself, "What is the worst that could possibly happen?" Rejection is a game of deception. When you visualize yourself taking a risk or moving toward something that sets off fear, the feeling is like drowning. You think you won't survive, and that death is near.

But let's get practical: What is the worst that could possibly happen? You have to remind yourself that life will go on. You'll live through it. You have nothing to lose (except pride and ego) so why not? If you don't ask, you lose anyway.

We often attach a disaster to the outcome as if, by getting a rejection, it is the end of everything. This fear is centered in the belief that we can't handle it. *"If they turn me down my life is forfeit."* I can tell you that life will go on, and the great thing is, you'll develop a mental toughness for it.

Step 4: Understand that rejection is an illusion. It is the ultimate lie that keeps you trapped. As long as you believe that you have everything to lose, you will be paralyzed with fear to do anything. I convince my subconscious mind that rejection doesn't exist, accept in my own mind.

Sure, we do get brushed aside, turned down, and told that we just aren't good enough. But that is the journey that successful people take. If you let a single rejection stop you from persisting, you'll struggle throughout your life to make anything work.

The power of the illusion is as strong as you decide it to be. You can let it defeat you or accept it into your life as part of the growing process.

Step 5: Keep on asking. Success is in the numbers: the more you ask, the better you get at it. It is a skill you can master with practice. You might only get one *YES* out of every fifty rejections, but it's better than nothing. And nothing is what you'll get if you don't ask.

Keep in mind that timing has a lot to do with your success rate. There were times I asked people for something once and they said *NO*; but when I asked again they agreed. Were they having a bad day when I asked the first time? Maybe they didn't need what I was offering at that time?

Persistence pays. Believe in what you are going for and ask with conviction. This will boost your chances of succeeding.

Step 6: Know WHO to ask and stop complaining about not having what you want. There is no point in asking a person who is unemployed for a job; they can't give you what they don't have. You have to ask the right people. What this means is, don't waste your time asking the people who have nothing to do with what you are going after. In addition, complaining to others about your hard fortune and not having what you desire will just perpetuate your situation of having less.

For a long time, I had a bad habit of complaining to friends and anyone who would listen about how I was always missing out. If someone I knew succeeded because they took the initiative and went after their goals (most likely by doing a lot of asking) I would be hit with jealousy and complain about how lucky he or she was. Luck had nothing to do with it.

The bottom line: stop complaining. You have no reason to complain and it can only do you more harm while building a wall of resentment. If you aren't taking action to get what you want, you can only blame yourself.

Step 7: Know WHEN to ask. Your timing can have a lot to do with the outcome of your asking moment. You wouldn't want to ask someone for a favor if they were in the middle of a personal crisis. For one thing, they are maybe not in a position to help you at that moment, or that particular time of day there is just too much going on. Observe and take notes. Know what you want to ask for and then watch for the opportune moment.

The most powerful approach is to do it with empathy. When possible, observe their situation and seek to understand the other person's emotions and feelings at the time. This could be challenging in a business environment, but every situation has its unique approach.

For example, how you ask your spouse for something would be different than asking a co-worker or manager. The level of empathy is different as well, but by measuring the situation and approaching when the timing feels right can deliver a better outcome.

Step 8: Know WHAT to ask for. One of the biggest reasons people go without is because they don't know what they want in the first place. You have to be clear about what it is you want, or you'll end up asking for the wrong things; or worse yet, you'll just take what anyone is giving away.

Remember: People normally don't want to give you what you want, especially if they still want to keep it, or what you are asking for is going to cost them in some way. But knowing WHAT you want will also determine WHO to ask. On the list of you made at the beginning of all the stuff you are going to ask for, now go back and fill in the name or names of the people who can give it to you.

Who can you reach out to today? Is there one person above all the rest that can deliver on what you want to have? Then you know what to do. But you might be having second thoughts. You are thinking they'll turn you down, or worse.

"We cannot become what we need to be by remaining what we are."

— **Max Depree**

CHAPTER 10

Simple Strategies for Asking

"Rejection can disappoint you, depress you and may even stop you in your tracks... learn not to take rejection so personally... if you're honest with yourself and believe in your work, others will too."

— **Bev Jozwiak**

Now, make a list of twenty things you are going to ask for today. Who are you going to ask? When? How much will you ask for? Be sure to be specific about what you want. Just "asking for time off" from your work isn't specific enough. You have to ask for three days or three weeks. Be sure that what you are asking for is **what you really want** and that it is **specific**.

When you go to the bank to apply for a loan, you don't just say, "Give me some cash for a car." You need to state how much it is you need.

Be **specific**.

Be **clear**.

Be **confident**.

Now, here are the nine strategies you can put into action when asking:

1. Keep track of your asking score.

Here is a tactic you can use when procrastinating on doing something. A friend of mine would keep two jars: one full of pennies and the other empty. When he took a positive action, such as completing a simple task or asking for something, he would move one penny to the empty jar. It worked because that simple action of moving pennies prompted him to do something every day. He said that he wanted to see how many pennies he could fill up the empty jar with.

Make a challenge with yourself and start off the beginning of the month with two jars, one empty and the other filled with thirty coins (or jellybeans or whatever you wish). Then everyday make a goal to ask for one thing you want. It doesn't have to be anything extravagant. Regardless if you get a YES or NO, you still win. The victory is in getting to the "ask" stage. Beyond that, the outcome doesn't matter.

2. It's a give-and-give some more.

When I learned to ask more and could confidently approach people about my desires to own, be, or do something, I had a great moment of clarity. When I received, I didn't just want to get more and keep taking. This isn't what asking is all about. You have to be willing to give as much as you earn, and even more. There will come a time in your life that people will ask you for the things you want.

I realized that what I received I was also willing to give away; but when I was rejected, or when I rejected myself by holding on to my "ask," I was less willing and kind to share with others. My rejectionism had created a level of scarcity in me that made me unwilling to give. I held on tightly and constructed a barrier around my life. Asking was another path to freedom and it can be yours too.

3. Believe you're worth receiving it.

For many years I shied away from asking for what I wanted. The reason was, I didn't think I was worthy of having it. Lacking confidence and low self-esteem, I would either take what was given to me, or learned to live with what I had. When you ask for something, you have to believe that it's yours to begin with. If you don't believe in it then who will?

One of the reasons we get turned down is because our approach is weak. If you are lacking confidence it shows in your attitude. You can't fake it. You are more likely to make a good case if you can trust in yourself that it is yours.

4. Develop an attitude of gratitude for what you get.

This isn't the same as "Settle for what you get." But the reality is, you might ask for ten dollars and receive five. You ask for a week off and you get five days. You ask for a kiss and you get a handshake.

We have to appreciate the fact that what we want isn't what people are always willing to offer up right away. Patience is part of the game, and if you lose your patience or turn from asking to demanding, you could end up losing everything.

5. Visualize your "big ask."

Visualization is a powerful technique that can prepare your mind for what it is going to do. It is so powerful that athletes, negotiators and presidents visualize the success they want to achieve and the outcome before taking action. Visualization is your mind training for taking action in the near future. If you can envision it, you can have it. Or at the very least, you can prompt your mind into taking action.

World-renowned actor and comedian **Jim Carrey** improvised a powerful visualization technique when he was struggling as an actor in Hollywood. In 1985, Carrey, with dreams of becoming a famous actor in Hollywood, wrote himself a check for 10 million dollars for "acting services rendered." He kept it in his wallet postdated for ten years. Carrey later went on to be paid millions for huge blockbuster films such as *Ace Ventura* and *Liar Liar*.

6. Visualize the engagement as a positive experience.

When I tried this for the first time, I would visualize the other person as becoming confrontational and angry. This created intense emotions of stress and anger. So, even when I did get up the courage to ask, I did it in a very aggressive manner. I wasn't asking but demanding. The other person, sensing this hostility, reacted in a similar state.

Under these circumstances, even if you get what you want, you'll damage your relationship with that person and kill any chances of future "win-win" situations. You might get what you want but at a price.

Visualize your "asking moment" as a positive, calm approach to the situation. It might not turn out the way you want it but going in with guns blazing is a sure way to kill any negotiations.

7. Know you have nothing to lose.

When you are gearing up to ask or approach someone, always tell yourself that you have nothing to lose: there is only a gain, even if you come away with a *NO*. Asking for things is like any other skill: it improves over time. The more you do it the better at it you get. You can only lose out by not asking.

One of the obstacles that creates hesitation and prevents us from taking action is the distorted belief that, if we are turned down, it'll feel worse than death, as if we have lost something vitally important. But, as I have stated, there is nothing to lose if you take courage and do something about it.

8. Know that the rejection begins in your mind.

Most of how we respond is based on our self-perception and understanding of the situation. If you get rejected, you can make it all about you and tell yourself it's because you are no good, worthless, and deserved to be rejected because you are unworthy. The other way to look at it is to see this as a moment where the person isn't ready to accept your offer; they are not ready yet, regardless of how badly or how much you beg.

People change day to day. What they want one day isn't what they desire the next. If you take rejection personally you are setting yourself up for future suffering. The rejection you labeled it as is all in your mind. You have to choose yourself in these moments and realize there will be other opportunities and circumstances to ask someone else.

9. Project your confidence.

You will have a much better chance of succeeding if you ask with confidence. Ask as if you really mean it and that you have already gotten a *YES*. People who lack confidence appear as if they don't really want what they are trying to get. The requestee picks up on this and is less likely to agree with your terms.

You can deliver this confidence before you even say anything. Pay attention to your body language, eye contact, and voice control. Do you sound confident? Do you look confident? Do you smell confident (people can "smell" fear)? Project the attitude of confidence with self-talk before you do anything. Pump yourself up and remind yourself there is nothing to lose.

You Get What You Ask For

When I was in college I had an interview for a part-time job on the weekends working on a construction site. In the interview the owner had asked me, "So if we hire you, how much do you expect to be paid?" I didn't want to risk not getting hired by asking for too much, even though I knew the work would be hard, so I gave a price just above minimum wage. I was hired and paid the price I asked for, which at the time was just above $6 per hour. I felt pretty good about that because I had negotiated my wages and the manager had accepted.

Several weeks later I found out that one of the other workers, who had been hired right after me, was getting nearly $2 more an hour! I approached the owner to ask why I was being treated so unfairly even though we were both doing the same job. He simply said, "I asked you how much you wanted. We are paying you what you asked for. The other guy is also getting what he asked for."

This was a powerful lesson that stayed with me for years to come.

You always get what you ask for. When it comes to the subject of rejection, as you already know, most of us will do anything to avoid getting turned down, even if it means devaluing ourselves. Another lesson to learn is not only will you get what you ask for in life, but what you don't ask for you'll get as well ... and that usually means nothing!

If you wait around for others to figure out what you want, you'll go without the things you really desire. Meanwhile, those that get ahead are seizing the moment and asking again and again and again for what they believe they deserve to have.

There is a saying: "Good things come to those who wait." I think this statement has a negative meaning—you might wait patiently for your day to arrive, for the right person to show up with the right opportunity, but it will come at a price. You could end up getting what is left over by those people who got there before you. "The early bird gets the worm" is a better expression to live by.

Think about all the things you are not asking for in your life. Chances are you could fill up a page right now. So that is what we are going to do, right now. Take out a piece of paper and make a list of all the things you want to ask for but have been afraid to. This can be anything from stuff at work to family issues.

Here are some prompts to get you moving:

- *"What am I afraid to ask my spouse?"*

- *"What am I afraid to ask my co-workers?"*

- *"What am I afraid to ask total strangers?"*

- *"What am I afraid to ask my neighbors?"*

- *"What am I afraid to ask my teachers?"*

- *"What am I afraid to ask of myself?"*

Everyone has something they are afraid to ask for. Once you clearly identify the things you are afraid to ask for, you can move forward with the next phase:

"Why?"

Next to the list of things you are afraid to ask for, write down the reason why you are afraid to ask. This is the fuel that will move you into taking action. Knowing what you are afraid to ask for is the first step because it makes you aware of what you are hiding from. But the *why* should make you at least a little angry.

"Don't waste energy trying to cover up failure. Learn from your failures and go on to the next challenge. It's okay to fail. If you're not failing, you're not growing."

— H. Stanley Judd

CHAPTER 11

Asking for Help

"Rejection is merely a redirection; a course correction to your destiny.

— **Bryant McGill**

When it comes to asking for help, there is a certain level of resistance that stands between you and the person you are reaching out to. When you ask another person to help you, you are leaving yourself completely vulnerable. It feels like you are giving the other party permission to take full advantage of you. How terrifying!

What if they say *NO*? What if they tell you that you're just not good enough to be helped? These sound like crazy responses to a reasonable request ("Hey, would you mind giving me a hand?") but rejection plays crazy games with the mind.

When you ask for help, especially for men, there is that stigma that says asking for help is the equivalent of admitting you can't do something. When you admit you can't do something it is the same as saying "I can't handle it." You might equate asking for help with being weak or incompetent.

But that's just not the case. Everybody needs help with something. And most people need help every day, but they won't ask for it. I can remember walking around in the large city of Tokyo once, looking for a certain spot. When it was obvious how lost I was, I had no other choice but to stop someone and ask for directions. Before I did, this is what was going through my mind:

What if they don't stop?

What if they laugh?

What if they say, "Sorry, can't help you."

It sounds over-the-top, but this is how the rejectee thinks. We run through a list of possible scenarios that lead to the worst-case scenario in every situation. And it always comes back to the same thing: "What if I get rejected? It will shatter me."

So, what did I do?

I did ask someone. The first person didn't stop. The next person I asked did. Not only did they tell me where the place was, they went out of their way to show me personally right to the front door.

Where would I have ended up if I hadn't asked? Lost and confused and kicking myself for not asking.

Asking for help, as terrifying as it can seem, is perfectly natural. In fact, when I think about it, I was always happy in any situation to lend a hand myself when someone needed help. It was a chance to be of service to another human being. By giving, you will receive every time, and if you don't receive anything, you are still ahead of the game.

You see, I was always afraid of asking anyone for anything. If I needed help with something, I would figure out a way so that I didn't have to ask. If someone saw me struggling, I would tell him or her, "It's okay, I got this." But the reality is, I wanted their help; I just couldn't admit it. I was always terrified that if I accepted help from someone, I would owe him or her something, and I'd never be able to pay it back. I didn't want to appear needy or incompetent.

So, go ahead and ask someone for help. Better yet, offer to help someone if it looks like they need help. Not everyone will ask for it and may even refuse it if you try to give it to them.

Here are some things you can start with:

- Ask someone to help you fix your car.

- Ask someone to help you lift something.

- Ask someone to help you with your homework.

- Ask someone to help you solve a difficult problem.

- Ask someone to show you the way to the hotel because you're lost.

- Ask someone to lend you some money because you forgot your wallet today.

- Ask someone to help you carry something heavy.

So, what help are you going to ask someone to help you with?

Now, it is up to you.

Draft up twenty ideas of things to ask for this week. You can also reflect on last week and come up with ideas on things you could have asked for but didn't. Chances are they will come up again.

One more exercise you can try is a self-analysis practice. Look at areas of your life that you are terrified to approach. This could be in a relationship, or a situation at work. Maybe you can't handle asking people for help no matter what. You fear looking stupid. Take note of the areas you retreat from.

Then ...

Choose one of your fears and focus on it. Think about how you are going to ask for this one thing. Feel the fear as it works its way through you. How will you ask for this? Who will you ask? When will you ask?

So, here is my simple 6-step process for asking for what you want:

1. Write down in a notebook or Evernote the one thing you really want.

2. Make a short list of three people who could provide this.

3. Write down the benefit you are providing by asking them for what you desire to have.

4. Ask confidently, as if it is already yours.

5. Be respectful of their decision if it doesn't turn out the way you wanted.

6. Finally, let go of your expectations.

You can make a massive difference in your life by asking the right people for the right things at the right time. Commit to asking for at least one thing you desire once a day. This can be something you want for yourself, or better yet, help someone else to obtain something they want.

Nothing happens in life unless you really want it. If you want it, you have to get out there and tell people. We can do this by asking for what is important.

Now, think very carefully about the one thing you want right now but you're holding back on asking for it. How are you going to ask? Who are you going to ask? When are you going to ask? To make it happen there has to be a plan. You need to decide what, where, and who. When you know this half, the work is already finished.

Create a Benefits Chart: Why Asking Pays

Create a benefits chart. On one side, you are going to list the benefits of not asking. On the other side, list the gains of asking. This is your **win-win** chart. Measure up both sides and see just how rejection is keeping you stuck.

What you can do is write down exactly what you want to ask for, and then how you are going to do it. How will you ask? What will you say? When will you ask for this? Interview yourself and get pumped up and excited about asking for the things you deserve and desire.

PART 3:
The Power of Desensitization

CHAPTER 12

Desensitization and the Flooding Process

"When you're not putting yourself out there, you're rejecting yourself by default."

— **Jia Jiang,** bestselling author of
Rejection Proof

You think you are protecting yourself when you avoid situations that are potentially harmful to your ego, confidence and pride. In fact, what appears as a protective cocoon really ends up becoming a personal prison created not to protect you but to isolate your fear from experiencing what it needs to in order to step out of the way.

In this final section of the book we are taking a look at how desensitization works and how to put it into action so you can numb your fear of getting rejected.

In *psychology*, **desensitization** is defined as '*the diminished emotional responsiveness to a negative or aversive stimulus after repeated exposure to it*. It also occurs when an emotional response is repeatedly *evoked in situations in* *which the action tendency that is associated with the emotion proves irrelevant or unnecessary.*

Jia Jiang and 100 Days of Rejection

Could you imagine putting yourself into a state of **Rejection Proof** where, for 100 days, you committed to provoking rejection in order to numb yourself to its negative effects? This is what Jia Jiang did in his Rejection Journey. Dubbed the "Rejection Whisperer," Jiang put himself on a quest to intentionally get rejected for 100 days as a way to overcome rejection by throwing himself right at it again and again.

Ever since he was little, Jia Jiang fantasized about being an entrepreneur. After getting a rejection email from a potential investor for one of his inventions that would launch his entrepreneur business, Jiang set out to "thrive in the face of fear," as he said. And the experiment was on. For the next 100 days, recording each attempt with his phone, Jiang tried some pretty crazy experiments in his attempt to get rejected.

Some of the best ways he would try to get rejected were:

- Asking a security guard for $100

- Asking to be allowed to make an announcement over the PA system at Costco

- Asking a hairstylist if he could cut her hair

- Asking a donut shop if he could have a special donut in the shape of the Olympic rings

- Be a tour guide at a museum

- Sell cookies for the Girl Scouts

- Find a job in one day

- Be a greeter at Starbucks

- Get a hair trim at PetSmart

- Challenge a CEO to a staring contest

You can check out Jia's website at rejectiontherapy.com and the videos that document his 100 days of rejection.

But, what is so important about Jia Jiang's social experiment on rejection isn't the fact that he did something that has rarely been done before, but that he changed and evolved from doing it. He learned with each lesson and attempt at getting rejected.

The lesson Jiang shares is critical to understanding *why* people reject you. You see, when you have a situation where you get turned down, told *NO*, or basically given bad news that you just aren't good enough for the "team," it feels like a personal invasion on your character. Think about the last time you experienced a really bad rejection. If you are like me it was like being stabbed repeatedly, but on an emotional scale.

In his book *Rejection Proof*, Jiang explains:

> *"I'd always viewed my rejection as some sort of rare disease like guinea worm, that inflicts terrible pain but only affects a tiny segment of the population."*

I can relate and I am sure you can too. But isn't it true that when you are experiencing some form of rejection, whether it be personal or in business, somehow it feels like it's all about you? That somehow there is something about you in particular that caused this and that nobody else is going through anything even remotely similar?

Let's look at it another way. If you perform for a musical audition and there are 500 performers, only one person is going to be chosen. It might be you and it might not be, but regardless, 499 people will be getting turned down. The same goes for interviews, dating, and sending in a book for submission to a publisher. Someone is going to get rejected. It's a relief to know that it isn't just you.

Jia Jiang also says:

> *"Outside influences have an enormous impact on the way people see a situation-- and those influences can change over time. The way someone feels about me, or about a request I'm making, can be impacted by factors that have nothing to do with me. If people's behaviors and opinions can change so drastically based on so many factors, why should I take everything about a rejection so personally?"*

We are sensitive people by nature. And rejection is the virus that has heightened that sensitivity to a boiling point. The fear we have that is labeled "fear of rejection" is really a deep and personal fear of ourselves. How "I" feel after getting rejected is ten times worse than what other people are thinking. But when it happens, shame kicks in. This, attached to a highly sensitive individual, makes everything that happens personal.

But as Jiang says, there are so many variables and reasons for not getting accepted that are way beyond our control. Beautiful, highly intelligent, rich, and powerful individuals struggle with the same thing. People who we look at and think "She has nothing to worry about" based on her appearance or social status.

But it comes back to this: I have yet to meet a perfect individual who was capable of getting everything they want or being liked by everyone. The next time you think so, check to see if they have wings on their backs, because everyone is vulnerable.

Everyone has defects. But we learn to deal with them. And, by focusing on personal development as a way to always make progress, you can combat your feelings of inadequacy. If you get rejected for something, you could ask for feedback as to *why* you received a *NO*.

By getting feedback and understanding more the reason for the decision, you can use that information to focus on tightening up a weak spot. I wouldn't go out and get plastic surgery if someone doesn't like the way I look, but, if it is a skill I can improve on such as public speaking, there are always ways to make it better.

You might feed these lies to yourself:

- *"I was rejected because I'm ugly."*

- *"I was rejected because I'm not smart enough for this."*

- *"I was rejected because I can't be loved."*

The list of lies goes on. But none of them are true.

So how do we get to the point in our lives where we can move beyond this illusion and start to feel better about who we are?

You already know the answer. From the beginning of this book we discussed how to choose yourself above any situation; how to tackle tough moments where failure was imminent and how to ask for what you want as a way of breaking that barrier.

But here is the thing. It isn't the fear of people that is the problem. For years I always thought that people were the problem, and if I could just figure them out I'd be less fearful of criticism and judgment. But it wasn't that.

Rejection rarely has anything to do with anyone else and more to do with how we feel about ourselves. As Jiang said, the judgments and decisions people make are based on their feelings, attitude, needs, and wants in the moment. If you don't have what they are looking for they'll find someone who does.

Understanding this one concept cuts our fear in half. When you look at it this way, you could say that rejection doesn't actually exist. It is a self-created condition that is rarely controlled by anyone else except yourself.

"When you give yourself permission to communicate what matters to you in every situation you will have peace despite rejection or disapproval. Putting a voice to your soul helps you to let go of the negative energy of fear and regret."

— **Shannon L. Alder**

CHAPTER 13

Getting Desensitized to Rejection

"There are two wrong reactions to a rejection slip: deciding it's a final judgment on your story and/or talent and deciding it's no judgment on your story and/or talent."

— Nancy Kress

When I finished high school, I had a job in construction and most of the work we did was outside. In the winter the temperature dropped to about minus fifteen or twenty. Those are cold conditions to be spending six hours a day outdoors working. But after a few days you got used to it. The first couple of days feeling that cold was intense, but over the course of a few days you never thought about it.

You'll get used to the conditions you are exposed to over a certain period of time and your body will condition itself to adverse situations after a certain length of exposure. Even today, nearly twenty years later, the cold doesn't bother me as much as most people I know. My exposure to harsh temperatures toughened up my mindset toward adverse conditions.

The same principle works for most things we fear, including rejection. We fear what we least understand, and if you are struggling with your personal rejectee issues, it is because you have been avoiding placing yourself in the path of direct fire. In other words, what we run from doesn't disappear; it just buries itself deeper. That which you resist, persists.

Facing and defeating rejection works in a similar way. You can reduce its power by conditioning yourself through exposure to rejection. This is what it means to desensitize yourself.

Desensitizing yourself to the fear of rejection is about taking action toward the events or situations that you fear the most.

Desensitization is practiced through conditioning your mind with repeated attempts at getting rejected. Based on respondent conditioning, it is a form of behavioral therapy used by psychiatrists to help people overcome deep fears and phobias. Also known as **flooding**, this type of practice can be used to condition yourself for rejection.

As we discussed earlier, **Jia Jiang** gives an amazing account of how he put himself out there to purposely get rejected over the course of one hundred days. His purpose was to get so used to being rejected that he no longer felt anything about it.

There is a lesson to be learned here that states: **What we do repeatedly becomes second nature.**

This could also be called **rejection mastery**. You get so used to it that soon it is no longer an issue.

Another interesting experiment that I tested is called Rejection Therapy, a systematic approach to mastering rejection originally created by entrepreneur **Jason Comely**. The rules of the game go like this:

You must be rejected by one person at least once a day. To be specific, you have to be rejected, not just try to be, but to do something that gets you turned down. If you get out there and give it a shot but your attempt at rejection fails, it doesn't count. Getting rejected is SUCCESS in this Rejection Therapy game. If your rejection is accepted, you can take it that you didn't ask for enough.

Can you imagine how you would feel after thirty days if you purposely put yourself in a position that challenged your comfort zone and pushed your fear of being told *NO* to the very edge? This is what desensitization is all about. You have been buying into rejection because, like many people, you spent your life trying to avoid it. By hiding from it and protecting yourself, you become weaker, not stronger.

Don't you think it's time to do something about this? I know I do.

What you can do right now is make a list of all the crazy ways you can get rejected. This can be a simple request; start out small if you want to. Build up to it. Let yourself get desensitized in small steps each day. Every day try and push the envelope a little further. See how many ideas you can come up with.

Then, at the start of each morning, choose the one you are going to implement today. You can make up your own rules for this, too. You can do it the Rejection Therapy way and count it as a success only IF you get rejected, or you can give yourself credit for trying it regardless of the outcome.

Creating Your Own Rejection Challenge

What ideas can you come up with to desensitize and reduce your fear of rejection?

Here are some things I have tried:

- I went to a computer shop and asked if I could borrow a computer for the weekend because mine had broken. Result: They said no, but that I could buy a second-hand computer for a very low price (at their store of course).

- I asked someone I didn't know if I could stay at their house for a week because mine was being renovated. Result: They said NO but offered to help me find a cheap hotel.

- I asked the police if I could take a ride with them in the patrol car. Result: They said NO but that if I went to the station and filed a request it would probably be granted. I didn't do that because I knew it was a no-brainer, but I asked something I never would have tried before playing the game.

- I went to an all-female Yoga studio and asked to join up. Result: They said NO (of course) but did direct me to a Yoga studio for men and women.

Challenge Your Rejection

Now, why don't you challenge yourself to giving it a try. See how many situations you can come up with where you are putting yourself in a situation with the possibility of being rejected.

Here are 10 fun challenges you can start with:

1. Approach ten people at random and complement each of them. This can be about something they are wearing, their style of haircut, or a personal characteristic you noticed.
2. Go to a furniture store and ask if you can take a twenty-minute power nap on one of their model beds.
3. Meet with your employer or boss at work and ask him or her if you can finish working thirty minutes earlier from now on to spend more time at home with family.
4. Tell someone it's your birthday, and ask him or her to sing Happy Birthday to you.
5. In a supermarket or café, ask if you can "skip to the front of the line" because you are "patience intolerant."
6. The next time you check in for a flight, ask to be upgraded to first class without paying extra.
7. Challenge someone to a staring contest. You have to hold the stare for a minimum of one minute.
8. Ask your manager or the CEO of the company if you can work in their office for the day because you feel it will help you become more productive.
9. Draw a picture. This can be anything. You can add color to it or make it as creative as you like. Then, carry it around for the day and whenever you meet someone, show him or her the drawing and ask, "So, what do you think?"
10. Ask a random couple on the street to tell you the story of how they met.

"Time and time again, we read that success comes from failure. Yet, in our own lives, we avoid it like the plague. We play it safe, never risking too much. And our souls shrivel in the shadow of mediocrity."

— **Jeff Goins**, Author of the National Bestseller
The Art of Work

CHAPTER 14

No More Excuses

"Just get out there and get rejected, and sometimes it's going to get dirty. But that's OK, 'cause you're going to feel great after, you're going to feel like, 'Wow. I disobeyed fear.' "

— Jason Comely

You need to take some small risk of the ego or else you'll stay where you are. If you don't, you'll have nobody to blame but yourself. Small steps make real progress over time. Taking no steps keeps you stuck. Even if you make small progress every day, it's still better than the other 99% of the people out there who are doing nothing.

Most people talk about the things they want to do, and they end up making excuses as to why they can't do them. Excuses are another way we keep ourselves trapped. You can free yourself by throwing out outdated reasoning that feeds the lies of what you can or cannot do.

- *"I'll do it when I have enough time ..."*

- *"I'll do it when I save more money ..."*

- *"I'll do it after I finish school ..."*

- *"I'll do it when the kids are gone ..."*

But those "some days" never come, and in the end, they live meager lives and forsake their dreams, casting aside everything for the hope of something that never comes.

Your excuses reinforce the possibility of being rejected. We make excuses because we fear negative consequences.

- *"What if it doesn't work out?"*

- *"What if they don't approve my application?"*

- *"What if I don't finish what I started?"*

- *"What if I get stuck?"*

- *"What if I fail?"*

I have always strived to make a better life for myself, but along the road I got stuck many times. I stayed stuck for many years, stuck in jobs, wasting time in dead-end relationships, hooked into various addictions, and spending my life like someone who didn't care very much for themselves. I wasn't just killing time, but I was killing myself, and my life.

The bottom line: **You owe yourself to live BIG.** There is no satisfaction in living small and staying hidden from the world. You can put yourself out there by choosing who you want to be and accepting who you presently are.

There are no more lies or illusions when you decide to take charge of your life.

When you choose to NOT believe in the lies, you are taking affirmative action toward an inner healing. You stop playing the victim and take charge. You can only do this if you make a conscious decision to evolve beyond your present state, which may be giving into your weaker state that keeps you stuck and trapped.

Put yourself out there. Take a chance and speak to strangers. Do the things you never tried. What do you have to lose? You see, one of the things that hold us back is in believing there is something to lose in taking a risk.

You are on a mission to engage in the total human experience by throwing it all on the line. Try the things that you are afraid of doing. You're not going to lose anything, I swear. You will only gain from it, even if you fail or are turned down.

Don't focus on the outcome. Drop your expectations. Expecting everything to work out is going to scare you into not doing anything. You'll suffer from **action paralysis**.

Here are some examples:

- You start up a YouTube channel to document your blogs or tell people how your week is going, make a mini-documentary out of it.

- You call up people that you would normally avoid.

- You talk openly with people about whatever is on your mind.

- You introduce yourself to random people at the supermarket.

- You tell your spouse and children you love them.

- You admit you are not perfect and you make mistakes.

- You try doing the one thing you swear you'd never do.

- You make it a daily habit to ask for at least one thing that you want.

Your conditioned response can be mastered through desensitizing and conditioning your mind to handle the bad stuff when it happens. You can, over time, condition your mind to adapt to getting told *NO*, "Get lost," "You're no good"; whatever people throw at you, you'll be ready to take it.

But the in the beginning it will be tough. Our fear of getting rejected is, like any fear, all-empowering until we strip it of all power it has over us. You have to prove to yourself the fear is a lie. You can instill in your confidence that all's right with the world and that you are going to get through this no matter what.

Here is an example. You have had an idea for a business that you want to start up. But you only think of it and never act on it. You're afraid of failing. What would it take for you to start up the one thing you have always feared doing? What would be the first step you could take? What would be the smallest initial step you could take?

We get overwhelmed when we think about all the big stuff. So, how about drilling down as small as you can? Not everything has to be taken in one big leap.

Think about where you'd be in six months from now and work toward a plan that produces real results. How would you feel in a few weeks if you suddenly took charge, put yourself out there, and started taking action on the fears that hold you back? I can tell you from experience: Rejection would lose all its power over you. In fact, you'd wonder what you were ever afraid of in the first place. But you have to start with something.

When you realize that rejection is less about you as a person and more to do with the request and dynamics of the situation, as well as how people are feeling at the moment, it becomes so much easier to just put yourself out there, it becomes easier to deal with.

It's just the way things are; we don't live in a perfect world. In a perfect world everyone gets along and gets what they want. In the real world, we know that isn't the case. In understanding this bitter pill of reality, we can look at our life problems and fears as less personal.

Toughen up and face the rejection that has been keeping you scared. For the most part, rejection is nothing more than an emotional response to a situation that you disapprove of or disapproves of you.

Action Plan: The 60-Day "Rejected on Purpose" Challenge

Here is what you are going to do. If you follow this system, within a few days and the weeks to come you are going to see that the rejection is only alive within you. It exists nowhere else. Nobody can reject you better than you can do it to yourself.

- Make a list of all the things you avoid because of your fear or anxiety around rejection.

- Now that you have your list, you're going to start doing these things.

- What would you do first if you knew that you couldn't be rejected?

A mentor of mine suggested this, and it was a miracle step. I had never done it before but after completing this simple action step, it was easy to look and see what I could actually do to overcome my rejected self. It was like a roadmap I had created, a checklist of sorts where I could go down the list and start checking things off as I did them.

Here is what you do:

Taking action toward the things that frighten you empowers your senses like nothing else. It pulls you out of that safety zone you have built to protect yourself. Your comfort zone is a cushion for survival. Sometimes we need the protection it offers; but most of the time we stay there and never make progress.

Just imagine how many opportunities you are going to create from today by doing the stuff that has always frightened you.

- Will you write a book?

- Will you publish a book?

- Start to interact with people more instead of shying away? (I am not referring to social media, but real interaction.)

- Take a job interview that you've been avoiding?

- Test-drive a sports car even if you don't have the money to buy it?

- Talk to someone that you've been avoiding?

Take action and take it every day. When you are fearful and believe you'll fail, do it anyway. Taking charge of your life is an action and not an event. You seize the day when you seize the moment. Nobody is giving you a roadmap to follow; the only map is the one you are creating today.

Will you live as a free individual?

Are you ready to be rejection free?

Action Plan

Take thirty minutes to come up with all the ways you can push yourself to take action toward something you normally wouldn't do. If your fear of rejection lies in relationships, you may have rejection issues with men or women. If your rejection issues are centered on acceptance, you might struggle to join in groups or events that center around community or social activities.

But there is a different variety to this game as well. In your daily life, make notes of all the opportunities you have to take a chance on something and you don't. You want to, but you hesitate because you are scared or you believe you'll fail.

Log these situations into your memory, and then make an attempt to challenge it. You may experience as I have that your rejection-centered self is controlled by fear in several situations. Once you identify what those situations are, you can then set up a strategy to take action in that area.

For example, I had a major fear of public speaking. I avoided it at all costs. So, I put myself in a situation where I had to give a speech and discuss something openly in public.

My other fear was meeting new people. With vulnerability issues, I made myself vulnerable. In the beginning I had a physical reaction to this approach with sweating and shaking. But after trying it ten times, I went from fear to desensitization of the rejection.

Try this and you will see it works. You can get the freedom to be yourself, and then, as you take more chances by putting yourself out there, you'll experience a new freedom you never had before. I remember having this feeling that the loneliness I carried with me every day was mostly my own making. Focusing on desensitizing strategies cured me of the pain of isolation.

For me that was the freedom I had always been after.

You can have that, too.

Building the Rejection Free Lifestyle

*"I think that you have to believe in your destiny;
that you will succeed, you will meet a lot of
rejection and it is not always a straight path, there
will be detours – so enjoy the view.*

— **Michael York**

You can create your own lifestyle, experience a transformation, or make choices that take you in a completely new direction. You are as free as you want to be. By challenging the fear and doing what scares you, rejection no longer has any power over you. You can gain strength from the power of thought, confidence, and pushing your self-esteem to new levels.

Before we part ways, I want to leave you with three final lessons from this book. But before that, let me say that this is a fascinating journey we are on. What makes it so interesting is that we are given so many chances to live life as we want to.

Three Final Lessons

Lesson #1: Tell Your Story

For a lot of years, I didn't think I had anything interesting to say. I was always afraid I'd be boring or people would dismiss my opinions or ideas as brining or unintellectual.

Then I became a good storyteller. I practiced telling stories in a way that engaged people. I did this not so that I could be more popular or get all the attention; I did it because I genuinely like people and want to share my own life lessons.

One of the biggest reasons for writing about rejection and sharing this experience with you is so that we can learn from each other's journey. Everyone has a story to tell, and it is essential that you get your story out there. You never know the impact you could have on one life.

Listen to the message that people are trying to get across. If you show a keen interest in someone they'll really open up and share their dreams and aspirations. This is the start of a good relationship.

Many relationships start off shallow and lacking any depth. People are afraid to get close or let down their guard. You can have the advantage by showing genuine interest and getting to know the other person through exchanging experiences.

Lesson #2: Put Your Flaws into Perspective

This is a book on self-improvement. With this material I hope that you have gained some benefit and can apply it to your life *right now*. Just take note that self-development doesn't mean self-perfection. We rejectees really beat up on ourselves. We ask ourselves for years, "What is wrong with me? Why am I so different?" You are not so much different. It's just that everyone else is trying so hard to be normal that it just feels that way.

We all have flaws. It's okay. You've live with these flaws up until now, and that is okay too. With this book I hope that you can overcome and manage some of your flaws; other flaws we cannot change, or they may take more time to heal.

There is no big hurry. You have time. One day at a time and you'll make it. You can accept yourself as you are, flaws and golden points. You might feel awkward or ashamed. But what are your good points? What makes you unique and valuable? List these out and remind yourself what they are.

Lesson #3: Take Action Consistently

Nothing will happen to change your fears, and in turn your life, unless you make the changes. To do this you have to be focused on the changes you want to see happen in your life as the result of your choices.

Do you want to stay trapped or break free? Will you explore the unknowns of your real self, or stay hidden behind a veil of fear that keeps you doing the same thing over and over again? Will you take action or wait for action to be taken against you?

The key to creating lasting change is to do something repetitively over a long period of time. It is the same with building habits. Do something for a few weeks and you'll gain some momentum, but if you stop, the habit you are trying to replace will return. You can start to **transform your life today** by taking some small action daily. Ask for something you want; take a small risk; read a book on personal development.

Stay focused on your path to becoming *Rejection Free* and you'll soon find yourself living a new life in different ways.

I know you'll do what is best. Do it for yourself. Do what you've always wanted to do but lacked the courage to move forward. Know that you can do anything you want to do if you have the courage to take action

Assess where you are at in your life and take that first step forward. Just one step will do. For today.

Small steps are big gains over time.

Ask for the things you want.

Help people get what they want.

Be who you are and not what the world thinks you should be.

You've got this, now.

You have a choice. Now go out there, seize the moment and live your life the way it was meant to be.

Life is too short to be scared.

Defeat rejection and live the *Rejection Free* lifestyle.

I'll see you there...

Scott Allan

"There is no failure except no longer trying There is no defeat except from within, no really insurmountable barrier save our own inherent weakness of purpose."

— **Ken Hubbard**

About Scott Allan

Scott Allan is an international bestselling author of over 30 books published in 12 languages in the area of personal growth and self-development. He is the author of **Fail Big**, **Undefeated**, and **Do the Hard Things First**.

As a former corporate business trainer in Japan, and **Transformational Mindset Strategist**, Scott has invested over 10,000 hours of research and instructional coaching into the areas of self-mastery and leadership training.

With an unrelenting passion for teaching, building critical life skills, and inspiring people around the world to take charge of their lives, Scott Allan is committed to a path of **constant and never-ending self-improvement**.

Many of the success strategies and self-empowerment material that is reinventing lives around the world evolves from Scott Allan's 20 years of practice and teaching critical skills to corporate executives, individuals, and business owners.

You can connect with Scott at:

scottallan@scottallanpublishing.com

www.scottallanpublishing.com

www.scottallanbooks.com

JOIN THE COMMUNITY OF 30,000 LIFETIME LEARNERS!

Sign up today for my **free weekly newsletter** and receive instant access to **the** onboarding subscriber pack that includes:

Begin Your Journey and Make This Life Your Own.
Click Here to Subscribe Today, or scan the QR code below.

Scott Allan

"Master Your Life One Book at a Time."

Subscribe to the weekly newsletter for actionable content and updates on future book releases from Scott Allan.